PRAISE FOR *OPENING DOORS TO EQUITY*

Tonya Ward Singer skillfully provides educators with a powerful professional learning model that is based on the most recent work and relevant research in the field. This book is a practical guide for making the complexities of teaching diverse learners more visible—to others and to ourselves—and for fostering rich professional conversations that are focused on improving the teaching of all students.

—Jeff Zwiers
Senior Researcher
Stanford University

Tonya Ward Singer's Opening Doors to Equity—A Practical Guide to Observation-Based Professional Learning *is a rich text for administrators and teacher leaders concerned with supporting the growth of others. It combines practical ideas to build a strong learning culture with ideas to take full advantage of "open doors" to move a compelling equity agenda forward.*

—Beate Planche
Educational Consultant/Researcher
Collaborative Learning Services

The writing, the depth, the flow, examples are all exciting and well done. Very appropriate for teachers. I recommend the book because of the detailed information, clear step-by-step process.

—Margarita Calderón
Professor Emerita, Author
Johns Hopkins University

Opening Doors to Equity *is extremely practical, clear, and easy to understand and implement. Most importantly, the practice supports sustainable professional learning of any content area or strategy, especially relevant now as we are transitioning to Common Core State Standards and in need of examining the effectiveness of the many new practices we are implementing.*

—Katherine Strach
Language and Literacy Consultant
San Mateo, CA

This book is a must read for principals, instructional coaches, teacher leaders, and others charged with the task of providing meaningful professional development for teachers. As a how-to guide, the practical suggestions within this book provide a relevant framework for implementing classroom-based inquiry.

—Judy Brunner
Clinical Faculty
Missouri State University
Springfield, MO

I recommend this book without hesitation . . . Gone are the days for teachers to be working "behind closed doors." . . . Go forth and TEACH like the world works—collaboratively with teams!

—Harriet Gould
Retired Elementary Principal, Currently Adjunct Professor
Concordia University
Lincoln, NE

Tonya Singer has compiled a cornucopia of best practice and top research under one roof in the learning community. The text directs and explains a culture where teachers assist each other in collaboration assisting students in growth and readiness for an ever changing world.

—Lyndon Oswald
Principal
Sandcreek Middle School
Ammon, Idaho

With all the changes taking place in education, this process of teachers working collaboratively together can both improve our instructional practice and open doors for us to support each other in ways we have not in the past. Both the improvement and support are vital in education at this time.

—Leslie Standerfer
Principal/Academic Associate (adjunct faculty)
Estrella Foothills High School / ASU
Goodyear, AZ

This exceptionally valuable book provides a clear process I can use to engage with my colleagues around learning. I appreciated the ideas and practical information that will ensure that my professional learning group focuses on student learning as evidenced in real lessons. The tools that Tonya Singer provides are useful and relevant, not to mention tried and true.

To ramp up professional learning, this is the tool that will start your engine.

—Douglas Fisher
Professor
San Diego State University

"Opening Doors to Equity *is truly a facilitator's dream. I could take it and use it well with teachers to engage in professional learning. The process is definitely tried and true— it speaks well of the author's experiences in real schools with real educators. On the basis of the amount of yellow highlighting I did in each chapter, I would say this is an incredibly powerful book.*"

—Lois Brown Easton
Educational Consultant, Author
Texas

Opening Doors to Equity

A Practical Guide to Observation-Based Professional Learning

Tonya Ward Singer
Foreword by Lois Brown Easton

A Joint Publication

FOR INFORMATION:

Corwin

A SAGE Company

2455 Teller Road

Thousand Oaks, California 91320

(800) 233-9936

www.corwin.com

SAGE Publications Ltd.

1 Oliver's Yard

55 City Road

London EC1Y 1SP

United Kingdom

SAGE Publications India Pvt. Ltd.

B 1/I 1 Mohan Cooperative Industrial Area

Mathura Road, New Delhi 110 044

India

SAGE Publications Asia-Pacific Pte. Ltd.

3 Church Street

#10-04 Samsung Hub

Singapore 049483

Acquisitions Editor: Dan Alpert

Associate Editor: Kimberly Greenberg

Editorial Assistant: Cesar Reyes

Production Editor: Amy Schroller

Copy Editor: Codi Quick

Typesetter: C&M Digitals (P) Ltd.

Proofreader: Dennis W. Webb

Indexer: Rick Hurd

Cover Designer: Janet Kiesel

Marketing Manager: Stephanie Trkay

Copyright © 2015 by Tonya Ward Singer

Printed in the United States of America

A catalog record of this book is available from the Library of Congress.

ISBN 978-1-4522-9223-6

This book is printed on acid-free paper.

14 15 16 17 18 10 9 8 7 6 5 4 3 2 1

Contents

Foreword

Lois Brown Easton

Sometimes there's much more to something than you think . . . much more! Open a tiny gift box expecting a trifle, and you may find a gem . . . or many of them. This is true of Tonya Ward Singer's book. I opened it cautiously when I was asked to review it; after all, it appeared to be about educating English Language Learners (ELLs) and I had never taught ELLs, didn't know much about how to do so, and didn't think I'd get much from her book. I was surprised when gem after gem rolled off the pages. This book does address the needs of teachers who work with English Language Learners, but it's about so much more: equity, in general, and the professional learning of all educators. She wants nothing more than for educators to change their attitudes, beliefs, behaviors, and selves in order to shake up our educational system on behalf of all students. This book was a gift to me, and it will be a gift to any educator who cares about all young people and their education.

The first diamond to roll out was the topic itself. Singer takes on a subject that still, somehow, resides like an elephant under too many of our tables: equity. She deeply cares about ensuring all students have opportunities, and she shares with her readers a motherlode of principles and strategies for elevating the achievement of all learners especially students in poverty, students of color, and ELLs. Her moral reasoning is as compelling as her logic: Equity is critical for the success of all of our young people. She understands the need for trust, and she dives in deeply to this sensitive topic to help readers explore their beliefs about differences and take actions to make differences into assets.

The need to continually reflect on our practices to address barriers that prevent some students from accessing content form the powerful *why* of this book. Like this author, I like to start work with the great WHY (a problem to solve, a passion, a purpose).

Singer does not mince words nor hide her emotions about the importance of equity in schools. She cares, and she wants her readers to care deeply enough to take some epic actions to make changes on behalf of all learners. Best of all—in the form of an assortment of minerals and gemstones—she shares hundreds of strategies for making changes.

Singer is ultimately practical. She understands the dilemmas of teaching, organizations, and substantive reform. For example, she offers two approaches to getting started on this important work. Throughout the book, she uses the language educators in real schools and districts use to provide details related to the most mundane things (but things that can block changes such as schedules and coverage of classes).

This book, in fact, is written at a level of detail that makes it immediately useful. It is oriented toward implementation. Not only is this book the "motherlode" of strategies, examples, and actions that are specific, readers can even access videos of strategies in action. So, if they want to do something about equity immediately, they can take one or more of the jewels from this book and make changes immediately. They can also, however, slow down and appreciate her superb logic, the way she deepens her case for equity and connects equity to all other aspects of the educational system, including school and district goals. Or, readers may want to read this book twice, once for the keen ideas and the second time for the inspired logic, the way she braids everything together.

For example, she braids the work of closing opportunity gaps with the work of professional learning communities (PLCs). Not only does she help the reader understand *why* changes need to be made to achieve equity, and *what* to do; she also understands *how* schools can elevate learning for all students, not just one teacher—and that teacher's students—at a time, but as a whole school, through PLCs.

The real gem in this book—shiny and large, perhaps an emerald—is the way it is written to be facilitated by either an outside facilitator or a teacher leader from within a PLC. It is, in fact, a facilitator's dream. Clearly, Singer has shared her ideas and strategies with others, perhaps in PLCs as a leader or participant herself. The Reflection Activities that sparkle in each chapter are just one example of how the book can help groups of educators learn together. The sections labeled *Nimble Facilitation Moves* shone brightly for me.

I found myself thinking, "I could definitely use this treasure of a book with teachers to engage in professional learning on the most critical issue they currently face—the lack of equity in our schools and systems." Singer's process is definitely tried and true—it speaks well of the author's experiences in real schools with real educators. Sometimes, for example, she focuses on what a facilitator might find difficult, such as helping groups address courageous questions that people raise—or simply getting them to raise those brave questions! It's also supremely helpful to have Facilitation Challenges and Solutions within the chapters. Her examples are authentic.

Singer takes on the classic facilitator's dilemma—the learning-doing gap. How do you help people go from their learning to making changes in real time and real life? She expects application and provides for it as a natural part of her strategy. She is relentless about cause and effect. "If only teachers did X." "The principal should have done Y." "Parents need to do more Z" "If only our kids had. . . ." Whose fault is it when a school provides inequitable opportunities to learn? What if things do not go well? Typical cause-effect thinking can lead to a deadening cycle of blame and shame, unless someone says, "Forget blaming and shaming. Let's just get on with this task of making school work for all students." No excuses!

Another diamond in this book is her overall philosophy. She embraces a growth mindset (Dweck, 2006) and expects that readers, too, will operate according to this mindset. Rather than seeing a limited world, Singer sees a world that can change for the better with hard work, focus, and learning. Her "can-do" philosophy permeates this book and assures the reader that equity can be achieved.

To extend my metaphor beyond belief, I believe Singer turned coal into diamonds in this book in terms of her discussion of observation, analysis, and sharing data from observations. Many educators assume that they know how to observe, analyze, and share their observations in the form of feedback. However, those who observe teaching and learning do not always know how to do so. They may focus on the teacher or on a checklist; they may record judgments such as, "Oooooh, this is a good strategy" or "That's a bad question." Singer helps readers understand observations that work because they focus on students, capture timing and quotes, and describe without judgment.

She also helps people understand what analysis really means. Analysis is a difficult skill, especially in collaboration with others. Sometimes educators assume that they know how to analyze something; in fact, they may be adept at the ranges of analysis, from "making nice" on one end to scathing criticism at the other, but they don't know how to be concrete in terms of their language, referencing what students are doing, and using language that can be heard. Singer provides a protocol as well as challenges and solutions related to feedback.

Singer's writing is personal, passionate, and pleasing to read, with rich metaphors to extend the meaning of her ideas. It is at the right level of informality and also credible and authentic. Singer is reader-conscious, providing readers with reminders about what they have previously read as well as what the "whole" is and how the parts fit. She then previews the content of chapters and ensures that her writing flows from the preview.

Singer does her best to warn readers away from her book: "Beware! This book is intended to disturb schools." But, do not be warned away. Consider this book a gift; open it and regard the gems that roll out. Although you will read, "If educating all students is neither your interest nor your responsibility, then you can stop reading, now, and donate this book to your school's professional library," confirm that you want to educate all students, keep this book, read it, and act upon it . . . and buy another copy for your school's professional library. Or, better yet, make this book the focus of your PLCs' book study. Actually, you should pay attention to this warning: "This book is best used when in community with others. Once the community is engaged, the system of schooling as you know it will forever be curious, disturbed, and changed." Be changed.

Preface

WHY THIS BOOK AND VIDEO?

Purpose: Equip educators with a model and a mindset for leading collaborative professional learning around live lessons to ensure diverse learner achievement in 21st-century schools.

Audience: This book and video tools are designed for all educators who strive to expand their impact on student learning by collaborating and/or leading collaboration to transform teaching. The primary audience is learning leaders including:

- Classroom teachers seeking to engage colleagues in deep collaboration
- Grade-level team facilitators and department chairs
- Instructional coaches
- Content specialists, literacy specialists, and ELL specialists
- Site administrators
- Curriculum directors and Title I program directors
- District administrators
- County and state-level administrators leading professional learning
- Professional learning consultants
- External support providers
- Professors of education and directors of preservice learning

As this book specifically addresses the role of facilitators, it also provides explanations, step-by-step protocols, video examples, and templates that are a powerful resource for all participants.

Content-at-a-Glance: The book begins with a rationale for *why* we observe together and then details in Chapter 2 the specifics of observation inquiry (OI), the model that is the central focus of this book. The remaining chapters focus on *how* via three stages: (1) prepare, (2) engage, (3) expand.

Prepare: Chapters 3 through 5 equip readers with tools for building trust and buy-in, engaging teams in identifying questions for inquiry, and planning the first lesson to observe.

Engage: Chapters 6 through 8 delve into the specifics of observing and debriefing together to deepen learning and transform teaching. Videos and training activities help readers both understand the protocols and facilitate others through the OI process.

Expand: Chapter 9 provides a big-picture look at the OI multilesson cycle and specific ways to facilitate deepening professional learning across the year. The book comes to a close in Chapter 10 with a focus on evaluating impact and expanding possibility across teams and into the future.

Appendix A integrates activities and key concepts from the book into a comprehensive agenda for a professional learning workshop that readers can use to launch OI in any school.

Acknowledgments

This book and accompanying videos are influenced by hundreds of teachers and administrators who have collaborated in observation inquiry (OI) with me over the past several years. Thank you especially to superintendents, principals, and teachers in the Mark West Union School District, Petaluma City Schools, Bellevue Union School District, Kawana Academy of the Arts and Sciences, Miwok Elementary School, Santa Rosa Educational Cooperative Charter School, Healdsburg Junior High, and the Mark West Charter School. Your work together for students is the inspiration for this book.

Thank you Kay Schultz, Ron Calloway, Fran Hansel, Tracy Lavin-Kendal, Jennifer Rush, Brigitta Hunter, and Lisa Ryan for starting this journey with me, and Jane Escobedo for collaborating to scale up the work in new ways. Thank you also, Jane and Jennifer, for forming a dream team with Matt Caamano and Kelli Matteri to share OI at conferences.

Seven teachers deserve a standing ovation for their courage and generosity in letting us film their collaborative learning process. Thank you Erin Earshaw, Corissa Sunde, Shannon Bardage, Jared Ives, Angela Werner, Erin Wilson, and Maria Stranzl for opening your doors to readers of this book. Kudos to Jennifer Rhodes and Steve Grossman with Klic Video Productions Inc. for an expert job filming and editing.

Thank you, Dan Alpert, at Corwin for believing in the power of this book long before I'd written the first word. I am honored to work with an editor so committed to equity and deep professional learning, and appreciate your spot-on insights.

Lois Brown Easton, I'm humbled by your inspiring foreword, and deeply grateful for your detailed manuscript feedback and recommendation for the book's title. I also appreciate the many educational leaders, listed on the next page, who participated in Corwin's peer review process. Your insights made a difference for the final product!

To the many authors I've cited, I appreciate your influence on my thinking and my work. Special thanks to Tina Cheuk, Elizabeth City, Linda

Darling-Hammond, Carol Dweck, Richard Elmore, Bradley Ermeling, Sarah Fiarman, Richard Gallimore, Claude Goldenberg, Bruce Joyce, Joellen Killion, Catherine Lewis, Aki Murata, Pedro Noguera, Rebecca Perry, Nikole Richardson, Maria Santos, William Saunders, Beverly Showers, Lee Teitel, and Jeff Zwiers.

I am deeply grateful also to Lisa Tamayo, Erin Beard, Pam Carpenter, Kimberly Greenberg, Elizabeth Lane, Cesar Reyes, Amy Schroller, Monika Scoby, Katherine Strach, Corissa Sunde, Codi Quick, and Sandy Ward for essential behind-the-scenes support and to JurGita Mazeika for photographic expertise.

Most important, I appreciate my husband Bill Singer, a dynamic teacher and loving father to our boys. Thank you for believing in me every time I embrace a challenge, and for sharing this adventure together.

PUBLISHER'S ACKNOWLEDGMENTS

Tonya Ward Singer and Corwin gratefully acknowledge the contribution of the following reviewers:

Sonja Alexander
Director of Professional Development, Educational Consultant, Author
Learning Centric
Ellenwood, GA

Judy Brunner
Clinical Faculty
Missouri State University
Springfield, MO

Margarita Calderón
Professor Emerita
Johns Hopkins University
Washington, DC

Margarete Couture
Elementary Principal
South Seneca Central School District
Interlaken, NY

Lois Brown Easton
Senior Consultant, Learning Forward; Independent Educational
Consultant, Educational Author

LBELearning
Tucson, AZ

Dr. Harriet Gould
Retired Elementary Principal, Currently Adjunct Professor
Concordia University
Lincoln, NE

Barb Keating
Elementary Principal Retired, now Educational Consultant
Formerly New Westminster School District
New Westminster, BC, Canada

Lyndon Oswald
Principal
Sandcreek Middle School
Ammon, Idaho

Leslie Standerfer
Principal/Academic Associate (adjunct faculty)
Estrella Foothills High School / ASU
Goodyear, AZ

Katherine Strach
Language and Literacy Consultant; Independent Consultant
San Mateo, CA

Bonnie Tryon
2007 National Distinguished Principal-New York
Principal for Instructional Planning and Support (Retired)
Cobleskill-Richmondville Central School
Cobleskill, NY

Marianne R. Young
Principal
Monument Mountain Regional High School
Great Barrington, MA

Rosemarie Young
Principal
Jefferson County Public Schools
Louisville, KY

For Mateo and Alec
May you always be curious and courageous in pursuing your dreams.

About the Author

Tonya Ward Singer, MFA, is a professional learning leader with a deep commitment to ensuring diverse learners excel with rigorous expectations. She consults nationally helping K–12 educators realize new possibilities in language and literacy learning to close opportunity gaps for ELs and students in poverty.

Tonya has taught at multiple grade levels as a classroom teacher, reading teacher, and ELL specialist, and has extensive experience helping school leaders transform learning at scale. Her choice work is supporting educators in launching and sustaining site-based, continuous inquiry around live lessons. She has been collaborating extensively with multiple districts developing, testing, and refining observation inquiry, the focus of this book.

Image courtesy of Jurgita Mazeika.

An expert in pedagogy for linguistically diverse learners, Tonya has coauthored curriculum for international publishers including Scholastic, Longman, and Oxford University Press. She thrives on leveraging research and innovation to solve educational challenges and inspiring others to do the same.

Connect with Tonya on Twitter @TonyaWardSinger, or via her website at www.tonyasinger.com.

Online Resources Included

Additional materials and resources related to *Opening Doors to Equity: A Practical Guide to Observation-Based Professional Learning* can be found at http://www.corwin.com/openingdoors.

1   A Call to Action

"In times of change, learners inherit the Earth, while the learned find themselves beautifully equipped to deal with a world that no longer exists."

—Eric Hoffer

Learning is a continuously moving target. When we learn something, it becomes the solid ground of knowledge beneath our feet. We can stand on it enjoying the confident state of knowing, or step beyond it to the edge of uncertainty where opportunity awaits.

This book is about leading students to that edge, continuously, by leading teachers to that edge, continuously. It's about facilitating professional learning to realize the vision that every child can succeed.

To transform student learning, we as educators must transform ourselves, continuously. It isn't a one-shot change, or leap across one gap from novice to expert. It's a leap across many, again and again. The driver fueling this work is our commitment to students and the question, How can we best leverage our actions to reach every child?

Everyone who has ever taught in a classroom knows there is no easy answer to this question. Some lessons flop. Kids respond in unexpected ways. Even when we find a powerful solution for one grade-level in one content area for one group of students, the variables change. What worked in one situation doesn't always work in the next. Instruction that is effective for many students doesn't always reach *every* student. And even when we do master the dynamic process of helping every learner excel *within* school, there is the larger question: Are we preparing students to excel *beyond* school in a continuously changing world?

What drives me is the belief that every child, regardless of family income, ethnicity, or home language, deserves to graduate from high school with choices and opportunity. This vision has led me to ask tough questions and continuously evolve based on the answers I find. A commitment to equity dares me to always look for evidence of my impact on *all* students, whether or not I like what I see.

Learning From Failure

Twenty-six fifth graders in inner city Houston first taught me the complexity of teaching for equity. After graduating with honors from a competitive university, I became a teacher and failed. My first year in the classroom I arrived at sunrise daily, and worked until the janitor locked the school each night. I prepped lessons at home until I fell asleep on my papers. Still I struggled to engage every student, let alone close opportunity gaps. Each failure fueled me with questions: How do students learn? What motivates each individual? What can I do to ensure linguistically and socioeconomically diverse students excel with rigorous content? How can we as educators shift the status quo of inequity to create true pathways to opportunity for every child?

Twenty years later, school leaders and organizations hire me to help them answer these questions, not because I have all the answers, but because I don't stop at simple answers. I ask deeper questions and help others ask questions. We get specific together about what we need to know about our goals, our students, and effective instruction to meet their needs, and then we collaborate to transform how we work to achieve our goals.

This book is about doing exactly this, collaboratively, in classrooms together to reshape instruction so that every individual child who enters our schools will graduate prepared to thrive in a changing world.

This is a how-to book for translating the theory of this vision into action in any school, and especially schools with one or more of the following priorities:

- Effectively prepare all learners to excel in a 21st-century globalized economy
- Elevate the achievement of traditionally underserved students including ELLs, students who qualify for free or reduced lunch, and students of color
- Build teacher capacity, continuously, collaboratively in high-functioning teams

These goals in my work as a consultant across multiple school districts specifically led me to the focus of this book, a professional learning model

I discovered by asking tough questions, learning from well-established models, and then transforming my ways of working, continuously to get results.

The mindset of problem solving that led me to the model is as important as the model itself. It centers on Learning Forward's standard that states "Professional learning that increases educator effectiveness and results for all students integrates theories, research, and models of human learning to achieve its intended outcomes" (Learning Forward, 2011, para. 2). Embedded in this standard is a mindset to design our approach based on the outcomes we seek, and refine our approach until we *achieve* those outcomes. This commitment to achieving outcomes and flexibility to synthesize and refine approaches to realize success is critical.

For this reason, I write this book with two parallel goals:

1. Equip readers with tools to implement observation inquiry (OI), a model for deep professional learning that engages teachers in a continuous cycle of planning, observing, and refining instruction together.

2. Fuel a mindset of continuous inquiry about impact that is essential for this or any professional learning model to make a difference for *all* students.

There is an irony in the combination of these two goals. With the first, I offer a clear path to follow, a means to an end. With the second, I provoke readers to question every means to an end, including the one I detail in this book.

In my work as a learning leader and entrepreneur, I've come to realize that one of the most important abilities for leading progress is the dual capacity to, on one hand, choose and stick to a path and, on other, to question the very path we are on. It's a difficult and humbling task to question our impact continuously, especially when we are committed to solving complex problems such as equity in 21st-century schools. Sometimes when we ask tough questions, we get answers that challenge us to change.

This book is about building that dual capacity among teachers and leaders who support them. It focuses on a model that brings teachers into classrooms together to observe students and refine instruction based on what they see. Before we get into the specifics of *what* with an overview of the model in Chapter 2, and *how* with protocols, video examples, and facilitation tools in Chapters 3 through 10, let's begin with the most important question: Why?

- Why is observing lessons together important for deep professional learning?

- Why must professional learning be as much about building capacity as facilitating collective innovation?
- Why do anything differently at all?

It begins with a complex challenge.

REACHING EVERY CHILD IN 21ST-CENTURY SCHOOLS

The challenges of teaching in US schools have intensified in recent years with a rise in expectations. Our 21st-century globalized economy calls for schools to prepare students for the workforce in new ways. Such pressures have led to shifts in expectations for students including

- adoption, in many US states, of Common Core State Standards in English Language Arts, Content Literacy, and Mathematics;
- new high-stakes tests with rigorous performance tasks: SBAC and PARCC;
- Next Generation Science Standards; and
- a call for 21st-century competencies including technology, communication, collaboration, creativity, and critical-thinking.

Even educators in states that have not adopted new standards or assessments are experiencing the rise in expectations, as the reality of our high-tech, globalized economy demands it. US companies looking for highly skilled workers often hire from other nations, as there are not enough qualified candidates graduating from our schools and universities. These trends are a wakeup call to the entire pre-K through university school system to rethink and redesign how we educate the next generation. Preparing students for economic opportunity means something entirely different from what it did 20 or 30 years ago, and will mean something different in the future than it does today. Changing expectations is a given, and schools need the collective capacity to adapt.

Complex Needs

Bring equity into the equation and our challenge is more complex. Even before rising expectations, we have been struggling as a system to meet the needs of underserved populations including ELLs, ethnically and culturally diverse learners, and students from low-income households. For some, grouping students into such subgroups is problematic, given the diversity of individuals across each group, yet this practice also has value for asking tough questions about equity and access to opportunity. Analyzing student achievement data by subgroups, a practice that became mainstream with No Child Left Behind, illuminates what might otherwise be invisible: troubling tragic correlations between demographics and achievement. A 2013 statistical report (Aud et al., 2013) from the US Department of Education highlights, for example, the following:

- Black and Hispanic/Latino gap data
- Socioeconomic gap data
- Gaps between NAEP achievement of ELL and non-ELL
- High dropout rates of black and Latino males

Teacher Expectations

Underperformance is not an indicator that kids in these subgroups are destined to underperform. In a profession where the majority of teachers are like me, white from middle-class backgrounds, underserved learners and the demographic groups they represent can be seen as *other.* All too often, even the most dedicated teachers may perceive data on the under-performance of certain groups as evidence that students within that group will likely underperform. Given the correlation between teacher expecta-tion and student achievement (Hattie, 2012), this is a critical issue to address. "Inside-out" approaches to professional learning such as Cultural Proficiency workshops and Courageous Conversations about Race are effective in helping educators identify personal biases and institutional practices that are barriers to achievement of underserved student popula-tions (Lindsey, Robins, & Terrel, 2009). This book takes a different, albeit complementary, approach in that it strives to meet the need for more spe-cific work connected to the daily teaching of rigorous content. In many schools, teachers are committed to equal opportunity and agree that high-expectations are important. The challenge is how they apply that global belief to specific daily practice: lesson-by-lesson, student-by-student. It often takes seeing students who have previously underperformed excel in a lesson for the "aha" realization that expectations need to be raised. It takes a shift from a fixed mindset that assumes intelligence is static, to a growth mindset that recognizes the potential in every student to grow smarter and more talented through effort (Dweck, 2008).

Equity Matters

Data about opportunity gaps are not just a call to action for all of us who believe in the promise of public education to provide opportunities for every child, it is also a call to action for all who want to ensure our next generation is prepared to thrive and lead a strong future economy in a globalized world.

The Organization for Economic Cooperation and Development coordinates an international assessment (PISA) to assess 15-year-old students' application of knowledge in mathematics, science, and reading literacy to real-world problem solving. International comparisons of 2012 PISA data reveal that US students perform on average well below students of other developed countries including Singapore, Japan, Republic of Korea, Finland, and Canada (Kelly et al., 2013).

Educational sociologist Pedro Noguera points out that US students' poor results in comparison to other developed countries in PISA reports is "largely about inequity-inequity in opportunity and background" (Kelly et al., 2013; OECD, 2013; Rebora, 2013b). The socioeconomic, cultural, ethnic, and linguistic diversity of the US student population is unparalleled in other developed countries scoring high on the PISA exams. Raising the achievement of underserved populations including students in poverty, racial, and ethnic monitories, and ELLs is critical for our nation's success. Noguera argues that as a nation we must "achieve excellence through equity." We cannot sideline issues of equity and succeed.

Shifting Demographics

Opportunity gaps are not new information, but they are increasingly important news for professional learning design as demographic shifts lead to increasingly diverse communities and schools. How we build teacher capacity to serve diverse learners including students in poverty, students of color, and ELLs will determine the strength of our national school system and future economy. Evidence of rising needs include the following:

Increase in high-poverty schools. Recent economic trends have widened economic gaps, and also lead to continued shifts in school demographics. One in five public schools was considered high-poverty in 2011, an increase from one in eight in 2000. High-poverty means that 75% of students qualified for free or reduced-price lunch (Aud et al., 2013). Even many schools that don't qualify as high-poverty have an increasing population of students whose families live below the poverty line.

Growing ELL population. ELLs are the fastest growing student population in the United States. There was an 80% increase in the ELL population between 1990 and 2010. As of 2011, there were an estimated 4.7 million ELL students in US schools, or 10% of the total school population. In my home state of California, more than a quarter of students in public schools are ELLs (Aud et al., 2013). While populations vary school to school and classroom to classroom, there is truth in Pedro Noguera's claim that "Every teacher needs to be a teacher of English Learners" (Noguera, 2013).

ELLs are a diverse group that share two factors: (1) some home experience with a language other than English—as indicated by a parent survey and (2) less-than-fluent English proficiency as measured by a school test. Beyond those basic similarities, ELLs differ in the following:

- Levels of English proficiency in listening, speaking, reading, and writing
- Home language(s)
- Levels of home language proficiency in listening, speaking, reading, and writing
- Academic and literacy skills
- Life and school experiences
- Racial, ethnic, and cultural backgrounds
- Family income levels

Many ELLs across the United States are also students of and living in poverty. Addressing the needs of ELLs in these contexts, including all of the schools highlighted in this book, often involves simultaneously closing opportunity gaps relevant to race/ethnicity, poverty, and English proficiency.

Academic Language Learners

Academic language is essential for equity and access in school and a key factor affecting performance gaps across different subgroups (Wong, 2004; Zwiers, 2008). Academic language, critical thinking, and content learning are intricately connected: We use language to think, to comprehend new concepts and texts, and to communicate. Many students, even native English speakers, come to school without experience using the academic registers of language prioritized in school. As a result, they are unfamiliar with the vocabulary, grammar, and organizational structures of language needed to comprehend and create academic texts and engage in discourse about complex ideas. Throughout this book, I will use the term academic language learners (AELs) to refer to students who have had limited opportunities to learn the academic registers of English that are central to school and career contexts. AELs include the following:

- Many students living in poverty
- ELLs at all proficiency levels

- Students who speak English fluently, yet only in informal contexts
- Standard English Learners (SEL) proficient in an English vernacular that is different from the English used in school such as African American Vernacular English, Chicano English, or Hawaiian Creole English

AELs are a diverse group of students including immigrants and nonimmigrants, students in rural and urban communities, ELLs and fluent English speakers, and white students and students of color. While there is tremendous diversity across AELs, they share in common an educational priority that is critical for access to opportunity: a need for learning academic language in tandem with content.

AELs need teachers who understand language, value the diverse linguistic resources students bring to the classroom, and effectively support students in building academic English for school and career success.

Teaching for equity is not a color-blind, culture-blind proposition in which we teach the best we know how and hope it works for all. It is about bringing race, culture, language, and poverty to the table, not as excuses, but as part of how we understand ourselves, our students, and ways to personalize instruction to meet each individual's needs.

Our Complex Challenge

A goal for equity in education used to be about helping all learners thrive in school. As a profession, we've reframed the problem from a broader perspective because success in school doesn't always transfer to success in a 21st-century economy. Creating equal pathways to economic opportunity is about simultaneously helping all learners

- excel with rigorous content standards;
- communicate effectively across diverse contexts and purposes;
- apply critical and creative thinking to solve problems;
- collaborate and communicate effectively;
- use and shape technology in a fast-paced world; and
- have the courage to risk, fail, and try again.

For students who struggle with literacy and academic language, especially AELs, this list of end goals does not change. Our task is to simultaneously build academic language and literacy while raising the bar across content areas and fostering competencies for 21st-century success. How do we leverage our impact to address this complex challenge?

Building Capacity for Change

Learning from schools that realize achievement gains, it is clear a systemic integrated approach of multiple factors is essential. In their report of a seven-year study of school improvement efforts across Chicago, Bryk and colleagues (Bryk, Sebring, Allensworth, Luppescu, & Easton, 2010) illuminated the importance of orchestrating essential supports to realize student-learning gains in reading and math. Five indicators they highlighted as essential from their findings include (1) school leadership, (2) teacher capacity, (3) student-centered learning climate, (4) instructional guidance systems, and (5) parent-family ties. They found that schools with strong measures in each of these indicators "were up to ten times more likely to improve students' reading and mathematics learning than were contexts where three or more of these indicators were weak" (p. 198).

While focusing on all five elements is beyond the scope of this book, beginning with this big-picture view helps frame my focus on building teacher capacity within a dynamic context. Building capacity must be about more than training individuals, and also about building relational trust, "a lubricant for organizational change and a moral resource for sustaining the hard work of local school improvement. Absent of such trust," Bryk and colleagues argue, "it is nearly impossible for schools to develop and sustain strengths in the essential supports" (Bryk et al., p. 207).

Beyond Silver Bullets

Equity in education is not a technical challenge that can be solved via a simple transmission of knowledge and skills from experts and researchers to practitioners in the field. It is an adaptive challenge that relies on changing people's habits and ways of working. An adaptive challenge "requires experiments, discoveries and adjustments from many places in the organization or community" to solve (Heifetz & Linsky, 2002). Closing opportunity gaps is such a challenge, as it requires educators continuously problem solve, study our impact, and shift how we work in response to what students need.

Workshops on strategies to meet the needs of diverse learners are a silver-bullet solution. This is the inconvenient truth the research makes clear: Workshops can work for transferring understanding and knowledge, but only shift daily instructional practice for a minority of teachers (Joyce & Showers, 1980; 1981; Wei, Darling-Hammond, Andree, Richardson, & Orphanos, 2009). Workshops are convenient, in high-demand, and great for business—but when it comes to impact, they are at best a shot of inspiration and introduction of new ideas into a system (Knight, 2011). They can be part of the solution to building capacity, but never should be mistaken as *the* solution.

I had my first "aha" moment about the limitation of workshops when I first began consulting a decade ago. When I sat down with a grade-level team to help them apply what I'd taught them in a workshop to their instructional planning, one teacher complained, "We can do this on our own, why don't you give us more strategies like you gave us in the workshop?"

To understand what she was looking for, I referenced an effective strategy that was highly popular in the workshop and asked, "Do you mean a strategy like this?"

"Yes!" she and other teachers smiled.

I then asked, optimistically, "Have you used that strategy with your students?"

Gazes dropped. Awkward silence.

Not one teacher had yet tried the strategy they had told me they loved in the workshop, and they were hungry for more. This team is not unique. There is a hunger for strategies, especially in field of closing opportunity gaps. Yet even as strategies accumulate in workshop binders on classroom shelves, the belief persists that if teachers just acquire more strategies, they will ensure all learners succeed.

Collecting strategies via workshops and books is the easy first step. Learning how to use them nimbly to ensure that every student learns is the challenge. Building capacity to address this challenge requires engaging teachers in continuous, collaborative problem solving around formative data to meet students' needs.

Collaborative, Continuous Learning

"Professional learning that increase educator effectiveness occurs within learning communities committed to continuous improvement, collective responsibility, and goal alignment."

—Learning Forward, Standards
for Professional Learning (2011)

There is a growing consensus among researchers and educators in the power of engaging in continuous, collaborative inquiry to improve practice (Wei et al., 2009). Countries whose students perform well above the international average on PISA exams, including Japan and Finland, build structures of continuous teacher inquiry into educators' workdays. In the United States, schools that realize significant achievement among traditionally underserved populations have in the core of their approach a culture of collaborative professional inquiry focused on ensuring students learn (Chenoweth, 2009; Gleason & Gerzon, 2013; Hollins, McIntyre, DeBose, Hollins, & Towner, 2004; Little, 2006; Saunders, Goldenberg, & Gallimore, 2009).

The challenge (as with the implementation of strategies) is translating this dynamic vision into action in schools. The growing popularity of professional learning communities across US schools in the past decade, for example, highlights some of the challenges of implementation. In many contexts, there was a shift in the name of collaborative teams, but not in approach. Richard DuFour (2004) pointed out, "The term [PLC] has been used so ubiquitously that is in danger of losing all meaning" (p. 6). He emphasized three big ideas that must be at the forefront of PLC work:

1. Ensuring that students learn

2. A culture of collaboration

3. A focus on results

These are no easy tasks in schools where opportunity gaps are prevalent, and current approaches are not meeting the needs of all learners in a school. Using data to determine intervention and enrichment needs, a core practice in some PLC models, is valuable and, in and of itself, does not begin to address the need for changes to core instruction. A teacher in such a context, for example, could work diligently to determine students' intervention needs without reflecting on changing how to teach. The difficult and essential work is to collectively use data to challenge our assumptions and drive continuous shifts in our teaching.

In their analysis of PLC work across 40 self-selected districts, Ermeling and Gallimore found a wide range of PLC practices and a troubling consistency: "an absence of talk about teaching and its improvement during learning community time" (Ermeling & Gallimore, 2013, p.42). Even teams working hard to implement workshop-inspired practices analyzed data to determine needs without leveraging that data in a reflective cycle of inquiry to change instruction.

These examples point to the challenges of implementation rather than a problem with the vision itself. Schools that function as strong professional learning communities illustrate positive impacts on student learning, teacher retention, and the working climate of schools. While a comprehensive review of the research is beyond the scope of this book, key sources include the following: Chenoweth, 2009; DuFour, DuFour, & Eaker, 2008; Gleason & Gerzon, 2013; Hord, 2004; Vescio, Ross, & Adams, 2006; and Wei et al., 2009.

As with many reforms, what matters even more than the name of what we do is how we do it. It's the ideas that matter, not what we call them, and our mindset of inquiry we engage in to continuously, collectively learn and evolve until we realize our goals for student success.

Courageous Inquiry

Everything I've learned about teaching, I've learned by asking questions and listening honestly to the answers, especially when they challenge me to change. Four essential questions that are central to inquiry throughout this book are

1. What are our goals for student learning?

2. What can students now understand and do in relation to those goals?

3. What learning opportunities do we need to provide to help students build from current abilities to realize the goals?

4. What do I need to learn or change about my practice to provide those opportunities?

On paper these questions seem simple enough, but in practice they are profound. Each is layered with nuances that matter in how we ask them and how we gather information to find answers. Goals, for example, can be as simple as standards in a lesson plan or an end assessment task we know students will face. Goals also reflect teacher expectations, a variable that shifts by teacher, can be tragically lowered by biases about student subgroups, and has a strong correlation to student performance (Hattie, 2012).

When we as educators ask these questions together with colleagues, and then take collective responsibility for applying what we learn to how we work, students win. Answers to these questions have the power to push all of us out of our comfort zone, especially when we ask them in collaboration with colleagues with a shared commitment to meet the needs of students now underperforming. When there is a gap to close between current student abilities and our goals, the easy approach is to attribute that gap to factors beyond our control, such as parents or poverty, and keep doing business as usual. The easy approach is to stop at Question 2, or change the pronoun "we" in Question 3 to the name of an intervention teacher, resource specialist, ELL specialist, or other we determine is responsible for helping our struggling students achieve.

Reflective practice begins when we ask Questions 3 and 4 with the courage to believe our primary job as educators is to impact student learning. In asking, "What can we do?" and "What can I do?" each of us acknowledges the cause-and-effect relationship between our actions and how our students learn. With this mindset, troubling data are our greatest teacher— an opportunity to transform how we teach and how kids learn.

> "To be guardians of equity we must ask tough questions and challenge patterns that aren't working."
>
> —*Pedro Noguera, Learning Forward Keynote 2013*

A RATIONALE FOR OBSERVING TOGETHER

Collaboration can be shallow or deep, a way to maintain business as usual, or a driver for collective change. To go deep together with the collective trust and courage essential for asking and acting on tough questions, we need to get specific with shared experiences and shared data. Otherwise, our conversations about goals, where students are in relation to the goals, and effective instruction hinges on our diverse biases and perspectives. We share ideas. We hear what we know. We miss a valuable opportunity to help one another expand our thinking and practice.

A Need for Shared Data

In many professional learning communities, collaboration only happens outside of the classroom. As a result, shared data are limited to that which can be removed from the teaching context: assessment results, written responses, or other pencil-to-paper tasks. Teams *talk* about teaching without experiencing it together. They talk about observations of student learning or challenges, without seeing the same thing. This is a critical point given the role of observation in understanding and addressing difficult-to-measure goals that are a priority for closing opportunity gaps in the 21st-century economy. Data for many of our priority goals live in dynamic moments of student learning and interaction. Consider, for example, what you would look for as evidence of student learning toward any of the following goals:

- Initiative and risk taking
- Problem solving
- Oral academic language development
- Academic discourse skills
- Collaboration
- Effective use of technology to research, create, and communicate

Written assessments alone do not provide the formative data we need to help students deepen expertise in these areas. To address such dynamic learning priorities with a collaborative, data-driven focus, teacher teams need to step into classrooms together to observe closely what students say and do, and then reflect deeply on the shared observational data to drive their collaborative work. Video is also an option for gathering shared observational data, but has limitations in terms of frame of reference, logistics, and trust, which I'll detail in Chapter 6.

PROFESSIONAL LEARNING FOR EQUITY

In the majority of schools featured in this book, building professional capacity centers on the goal of elevating the academic achievement of linguistically and culturally diverse learners and children from low-income households. Some schools are Title I with high concentrations of students who are AELs including ELLs, students of color, and students living in poverty. Other schools have great socioeconomic diversity and a small, growing population of AELs. Each of these schools has made it a priority to help mainstream teachers elevate achievement for students who are underperforming, specifically AELs. Shared goals for professional learning include building teacher commitment and capacity to

- raise expectations for achievement of all students;
- elevate students' active engagement across all lessons;
- teach language in tandem with content and critical thinking;
- elevate students' oral academic language use and collaborative conversation skills; and
- deepen expertise in using formative data to refine instruction to meet the needs of all learners.

Initially, when teachers only collaborated to address these goals via meetings, their conversations about observation data specific to these goals remained general, or worse tipped toward low-expectation descriptions about what "my students can't do." Without seeing the same students or lessons, colleagues lacked the data to drive a deeper discussion. Conversations thus centered on individual interpretations of what each teacher saw alone. In a staff room conversation, for example, teachers might say,

"I tried pair-share and it didn't work."

or

"When I tried to structure a deep conversation about the reading, my ELL students were quiet."

Listening to such statements in a conversation, each of us imagines something different based on our experience of what pair-share looks like, or the reasons a student might not participate in a classroom conversation. We could brainstorm ideas together for addressing these challenges, and it might be somewhat helpful, but without shared data our conversation isn't precise enough about the problem or the specifics of the solution to likely change how any of us work. The deep collaboration begins when we plan together how to address a challenge, and test and refine it via a cycle of planning, observing, and reflecting on what we see. In those instances, we have shared data about the context of instruction and what students say and do throughout the learning experience. Such specificity helps us move away from biased statements such as, "my students can't do that" toward precise insights about what students can do and need to learn. Specificity also helps us see the impact of our instructional moves and change our approach in nuanced ways as needed to realize our vision for student success.

Language, Literacy, Content

> *"A focus on language is crucial, no matter what subject is being taught . . . Teachers must know enough about language to discuss it and support its development with students."*

> Fillmore & Snow (2000)

Ensuring AELs access rigorous academic learning requires teachers teach language in tandem with content (Gibbons, 2009; Goldenberg & Coleman, 2010; Santos, Darling-Hammond, & Cheuk, 2012; Zwiers, O'Hara, & Pritchard, 2014). This requires understanding of the language demands of curriculum, student language use, and effective pedagogy for supporting language development in the context of rigorous academic tasks. Building these understandings in collaboration is no easy task, as language is complex to understand and define. A recent TESOL report illustrates this challenge, "When educators—including ESL teachers—talk about language, it is not always clear that they agree on the ways that they conceptualize language or what it means to provide language instruction" (Valdés, Kibler, & Walqui, 2014, p. 20).

Shared understandings and shared data are essential for collaboration to impact teaching and learning. To get specific about goals, student language use, and effective pedagogy for building academic language in tandem with content, educators must step into classrooms together and learn from the specifics of dynamic classroom interactions. See Figure 1.1 for examples of essential questions about the goal, students, and instruction we can only answer in tandem with observing students in action.

Teaching language in tandem with content requires continuous inquiry about what language students know and what they need to

Figure 1.1   Sources of Formative Data on Academic Language and Discourse

	Out of the Classroom	In the Classroom
1. What is our goal for student learning?	What are the language demands of our content learning goal, task(s), and reading(s)? What discourse skills do students need to excel in related collaboration tasks?	What does a proficient academic response specific to this context sound like? What does proficient academic discourse specific to this context sound like?
2. What can students understand and do in relation to the goal? (Formative data)	What does students' academic writing tell us about their strengths and instructional needs with language, literacy, and content learning?	What do students say in specific academic contexts? How do they use language? What discourse moves do they use in academic conversations? Do students take turns answering the same question, or build up ideas together?
3. What opportunities do we need to provide to help students close the gap? (Instruction)	What approaches do researchers and experts in the field recommend? What is working in other schools?	What instructional approaches elevate student's understanding and use of academic language in our classrooms? What approaches are most effective for engaging all students in academic discussions? How do shifts in scaffolds, modeling, or task structure impact students' academic language use, content understanding, critical thinking, or participation?

know to excel with the academic content we teach (Santos et al., 2012). Language demands are dynamic and change across different contexts and purposes. As a result, even when teachers know what academic language students know and need to know in one context, the rules will change in a different lesson with different tasks. Add to this the complexity of diverse language proficiencies among students in every classroom, and it becomes clear why there is no "silver bullet" approach to teaching language and content together. Effective teachers of AELs are data-gatherers and problem solvers—always shifting the level of scaffolds they provide to balance support with rigor, foster independence, and engage every learner every time.

Using Formative Data to Drive Teaching

How teachers interpret and respond to what students say and do in the moment of learning determines their impact. How teachers interpret students' use of language and adjust instruction according to needs is central to their effectiveness as teachers of AELs. In most classrooms, teachers are alone to refine this art. Professional learning designs must shift this trend, especially in linguistically diverse schools, as teachers need opportunities to deepen expertise analyzing and acting on observational data. "Teachers' skills in drawing inferences from students' responses are crucial to the effectiveness of formative assessment" asserts formative assessment expert Margaret Heritage. "In essence, teachers need to infer what 'just the right gap' is between current learning and desired goals, identifying students' emerging understanding or skills so they can build on these by modifying instruction to facilitate growth" (Heritage, 2007, p. 144). Collaborating in inquiry in cycles of planning, observation, and reflection builds the collective capacity of teacher teams to use formative data strategically to refine instruction according to students' diverse and evolving needs.

A Need for Collaborative Innovation

Formal educational research does not keep pace with the continuously evolving challenge for educators to solve. While there is a strong research base for many practices in the teaching of reading, for example, research specific to the long-term achievement of AELs is limited. Even when we narrow the scope from AELs to ELLs, there is a significant lack in conclusive findings to drive practice. In their 2010 book *Promoting Academic Achievement Among English Learners: A Guide to the Research,* Goldenberg and Coleman point out there is virtually no research to conclude the following:

- How classroom instruction might best promote oral language development (Genesee, Lindholm-Leary, Saunders, & Christian, 2006)
- The superiority of any approach to English Language Development
- How to ensure ELLs gain increasing access to grade-level curriculum

Most practices in these areas are based on theories, assumptions, and/or recommendations from experts. The same is true for practices for ensuring students excel with 21st-century competencies including critical thinking and innovation, and for practices integrating new technology into classrooms. At the cutting edge, research does not pave the forward path. This dearth of proven practices presents a challenge for educators and an opportunity for every teacher team across the nation to be at the forefront

What is unique about OI is how it integrates effective design features into a concrete model that directly supports teachers in collaborating to elevate learning for culturally and linguistically diverse students across a school year.

In this chapter, we'll explore the OI model including its roots and unique features in these five sections:

1. Overview

2. Collaborative Inquiry in Classrooms Together

3. Multiple Cycles to Experiment and Evolve

4. Protocols to Foster Deep Learning

5. Getting Started

The first four address the question, What is OI? The last section launches the how-to focus of the rest of the book with logistical considerations about participation and scheduling for getting started.

OBSERVATION INQUIRY OVERVIEW

When introducing any learning model involving team observations to educators who don't yet open their doors to observing together, it is effective to keep the initial introduction brief. The at-a-glance overview of OI is a helpful tool for this purpose. (See page 21.) At the first introduction of the idea of observing lessons together, plan to immediately delve into the activities outlined in Chapter 3 to address fears and build trust. In this book, we take a different approach by putting the elephant of emotion on hold until the next chapter, and fueling the intellect now with a more detailed explanation of the mode including influences and key distinctions from other learning designs.

As you read the at-a-glance overview, consider the following questions:

- How is this approach similar to or different from other professional learning designs?
- What are the features of this learning design?
- How does each support adult learning and shifts in teaching practice?

Comparing Design Features at a Glance

OI involves an integration of design features from influential models, especially, Lesson Study (Ermeling & Graff-Ermeling, 2014; Lewis, Perry,

Observation Inquiry at a Glance

Teams: Three to eight colleagues that teach the same grade level, subject area, or share a common focus form a team.

Focus: Teams identify a problem of practice (POP) they are driven to address together to make significant impact on student engagement and learning.

Launch: Facilitators launch the process with 6 to 9 professional learning hours to help participants

- build buy-in and trust;
- identify a data-driven focus;
- plan pre/postassessment;
- learn and practice protocols;
- schedule logistics; and
- plan the first lesson.

Inquiry cycle: In a school year, teams engage in four or five half-days of inquiry around live lessons, each scheduled about one month apart and taught by a different member of the team. In each inquiry cycle, one teacher teaches a lesson the team has planned while observers take notes on student actions and speech relevant to the POP. Using a nonevaluative protocol, the team discusses and analyzes student learning. They build on insights to set individual and team goals and to plan the next lesson for inquiry.

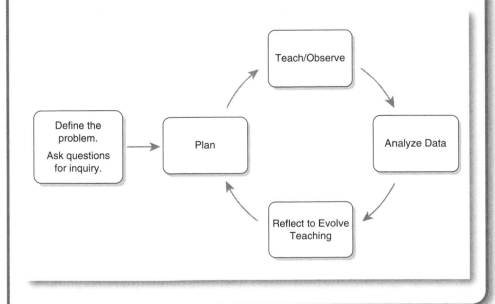

& Murata, 2006), teacher inquiry (Gallimore et al., 2009), Instructional Rounds (City et al., 2009), and peer coaching (Moran, 2007; Killion et al., 2012). Figure 2.1 highlights key similarities and differences between OI and each influential professional learning design.

Figure 2.1 Observation Inquiry in Comparison to Other Models

Influential Model	Shared Features	Differences in Observation Inquiry (OI)
Lesson Study	Data-driven inquiry on a shared goal for student learning Teams plan, teach, observe, reflect, and refine instruction together.	Less time on lesson development, more time in trial and error cycle of testing approaches, gathering observational data, and refining teaching together across four or five lessons in a year. Each lesson is in a new classroom with a different teacher. All team members take a turn teaching a team-planned lesson in the year. Protocol to debrief lessons builds in structured steps from description, to analysis, to action. Personal goal setting and shared accountability to apply learning to every team-members' classroom.
Team Inquiry Teams in a PLC	Continuous, collaborative data-driven inquiry to advance student and teacher learning	In OI, formative data always includes shared observational data. Teams plan, teach, observe, reflect on, and refine instruction together.
Instructional Rounds/ Teacher Rounds	Observation of lessons Structured debrief protocol	In OI, all observers have planned the lesson as a team. Inquiry focus is specific to a team-level POP and how teacher actions impact student learning (versus the leadership question of how site/district initiatives impact instruction and learning).
Peer Coaching	Observation of lessons Personal reflection and goal setting Accountability	No hierarchy of roles, even when facilitator brings content expertise. All members are learners and problem solvers together.

In the next three sections of this chapter, we'll explore the essential design features and nuanced comparisons to other models within three big ideas:

1. Collaborative inquiry in classrooms together

2. Multiple cycles to experiment and evolve

3. Protocols to foster deep learning

COLLABORATIVE INQUIRY IN CLASSROOMS TOGETHER

Observation Inquiry involves a synthesis of design elements beginning with a shared focus on a problem to solve, question to research, or goal to achieve.

Shared Focus to Solve a Problem of Practice

Focus matters, especially in education where time is a valuable commodity and there are complex challenges to solve. In OI, teams focus their ongoing collaboration on a POP they determine is a high priority to solve both to elevate student learning and deepen teacher expertise. This focus also connects intentionally to site/district initiatives in a way that is directly relevant to the team's students and curriculum goals. POP examples include the following:

- Students often demonstrate literal comprehension in reading assessments and classroom discussions, but struggle to make inferences and support their thinking with textual evidence. Many only retell literal details in speaking and writing tasks that require critical analysis of texts. (Upper elementary team focused on literacy)

- When asked open-ended questions that elicit high-level thinking, many of our long-term English Learners struggle to respond. Some take a passive role in classroom discussions. Others participate, but express their ideas using short sentences. Teachers find it challenging to integrate high-level discussions into daily lesson plans and to manage those discussions so all participate deeply. (Cross-disciplinary middle school team focused on ELL achievement)

Collaborating to solve a specific POP is rooted in many professional learning models including teacher inquiry (Gallimore et al., 2009), Instructional Rounds (City et al., 2009), Teacher Rounds (Del Prete, 2013), and with nuanced differences in name and concept, Lesson Study (Ermeling & Graff-Ermeling, 2014; Lewis et al., 2006), and Action Research (Mitchell, Reilly, & Logue, 2009; Richardson, 2000). See Chapter 5 for detailed examples, strategies, and facilitation tools for identifying a problem and inquiry questions to drive deep collaborative work.

Collaborative Inquiry Centered on Student Data

Inquiry is the practice of asking questions to deepen understanding or solve a problem. It's central to the human pursuit of understanding and innovation across diverse contexts including scientific research, engineering design, and business innovation. Professional learning models that center on inquiry include Action Research (Mitchell et al., 2009; Richardson, 2000), Instructional Rounds (City et al., 2009), Teacher Rounds (Del Prete, 2013), Lesson Study (Ermeling & Graff-Ermeling, 2014; Lewis et al., 2006), and Teacher Inquiry (Gallimore et al., 2009).

The steps in OI share many similarities to other approaches to human inquiry in the fields of education, science, engineering, and business. While humans name the stages of inquiry differently in different contexts, core features are the same. Figure 2.2 compares the steps of OI to two other frameworks for inquiry and innovation.

1. Essential science and engineering practices defined in the Next Generation Science Standards (NGSS Lead States, 2013)

2. Design Thinking, a mindset, approach, and set of tools used in many organizations for problem solving and innovation (Fast Company Staff, 2006; IDEO, 2013)

Each of these approaches is unique in purpose, procedure, and approach, and yet they all share at the core what matters most for human learning and innovation: inquiry.

As you analyze Figure 2.3, reflect on the similarities across the three models for inquiry. Why are these essential features for any professional learning design focused on continuous improvement?

More Than Steps on Paper

Inquiry is more of a practice and mindset than a lockstep process. Even when we chart the steps of inquiry in a series of steps as in Figure 2.3, it is important to remember that pursing solutions to unsolved problems, and answers to unanswered questions is inherently messy. Failure is a given when we engage in trial and error. At the moment of failure, when an

Figure 2.2   Steps for Inquiry Across Three Models

Observation Inquiry	Scientific Practices in Next Generation Science Standards	Design Thinking (IDEO, 2013)
1. Define a problem to solve. Ask questions to drive inquiry.	SP1. Ask questions (science) and define problems (engineering).	Discovery. Interpretation.
2. Research to plan a theory of action.	SP2. Develop and use models.	Ideation.
3. Plan a lesson to test an approach.	SP3. Plan and carry out investigations.	Experimentation. Make prototypes.
4. Teach and observe.	SP4. Analyze and interpret data.	Get feedback.
5. Analyze and interpret observation data.		
6. Analyze impact to reflect on and refine teaching.	SP6. Construct explanations (science) and design solutions (engineering).	Evolution.
Repeat inquiry cycle: plan, teach/observe, analyze, and reflect.	Repeat inquiry cycle: ask, investigate, analyze, and design/explain.	Repeat experimentation-evolution cycle.

approach we predicted would solve a problem doesn't work, inquiry feels anything but linear. Data we didn't anticipate challenge our assumptions. It drops an insurmountable wall in the path assumed would work to find a solution and forces us to find another way. We end up with more questions than answers or new, more clearly defined problems to solve.

Failure is a good thing. In his book, *Ignorance: How it Drives Science*, Stuart Firestein (2012) points out that the most significant breakthroughs in science often come from experiments that don't go as expected. In teaching, we also often learn the most from lessons that don't go as planned. When what we expect to work works, there is something to celebrate. When what we expect to work doesn't work, there is something to learn. In collaborative inquiry, our goal is to push beyond what we are sure will work by asking questions to which we don't know the answer, questions that catapult us into that tenuous space of risking failure and discovering data that challenges us to think and act in new ways. This courageous mindset is everything. Following steps of an inquiry model, without being at this edge, won't lead to learning or innovation.

Team Planning, Observation, and Analysis of Live Lessons

Lesson Study, a practice originating in Japan, is the most widely known model for engaging educators in collaborative inquiry around live lessons. It is also the primary inspiration for OI, and thus shares essential design features. In Lesson Study, educators collaborate to create a detailed research lesson in which one team-member then teaches as colleagues and invited guests take notes and gather evidence of student learning and thinking. In a formal reflection meeting, observers reflect on the lesson, and the team usually follows up to revise it for a second research lesson in the year (Ermeling & Graff-Ermeling, 2014; Lewis, Perry, Friedkin, & Roth, 2012; Lewis, 2002; Lewis et al., 2006). Lesson Study also has its own norms, timelines, and expectations that are distinct from OI. It is a powerful model that I recommend educators continue to use in any context where the design is a match for professional learning resources and goals.

To maintain clarity about the meaning of "Lesson Study" with respect to the original Japanese model, I intentionally avoid using that term to describe this work. It's ultimately a matter of semantics whether we define OI as a lesson study adaptation or as a new model. Either way, the specific design of this model will be of interest to educators studying ways to apply the concept of Lesson Study into new contexts for professional learning, especially to elevate achievement of students in poverty, students of color, and ELLs in rigorous 21st-century learning contexts.

What is unique about OI are design shifts we made to address language and literacy goals, increase collective responsibility, and improve the transfer from team inquiry to individual instruction. These key differences, and their roots in learning theory and/or other learning designs, are the focus of the next sections of this chapter.

MULTIPLE CYCLES TO PLAN-TEACH-OBSERVE-REFLECT-PLAN

One distinction between OI and Japanese Lesson Study is the time emphasis and number of lessons a team studies in a year. Japanese Lesson Study usually involves multiple collaborative meetings to design the research lesson, an advantageous approach for detailing a coherent lesson narrative, anticipated student responses, and observation priorities (Ermeling & Graff-Ermeling, 2014). Following the research lesson, the team meets additional times to plan lesson revisions and often does a second research lesson. In OI, teams engage in a similar flow of events with a distinct time difference: less time planning the first lesson and more time in classrooms together in the trial-and-error cycle of teaching, observing, and reflecting. In 18 hours of professional learning time, for example, teachers in lesson study would plan-teach-observe-refine two lessons, and teachers in OI would plan-teach-observe-refine four lessons.

Differences in planning emphasis and structure are not simply a question of quality versus quantity. Each approach has advantages, depending on the outcome goals and resources for professional learning. Benefits of engaging teachers in a multiple-lesson inquiry cycle within one year include the following:

- Shared ownership and accountability to each teach a lesson
- A sustained focus to elevate student learning
- Multiple feedback loops to foster risk taking and innovation
- Increased opportunities to identify students' specific needs
- Structured time to apply insights to individual teaching
- Deep learning through application across diverse contexts

Shared Ownership and Accountability

Teachers on a team take turns teaching the team-planned lesson. This means that in teams of five or fewer members, every teacher has an opportunity to teach as colleagues observe. This fosters a "we are all in this together" mindset that lowers anxiety and builds camaraderie throughout the process. When all observers will have a turn opening doors to colleagues, all have an active investment in helping the team follow norms and protocols that make the process safe. Shared ownership in teaching lessons also creates shared accountability to apply learning from the team process to their classrooms. As one teacher explained, "In the first lessons when I was an observer, I knew I had to apply what we were learning to my classroom even then—so I could keep up with the team conversations, and also ensure my students were going to be ready for the next level of learning when it was our turn."

Sustained Focus to Elevate Student Learning

Professional learning activities that are sustained and intense have the greatest impact on student outcomes (Little, 2006; Wei et al., 2009). The multilesson cycle engages teachers in a continuous focus in a specific area relevant to their content, their students, and district goals. As teams collaboratively plan, observe, and reflect on multiple lessons, their conversations move from general-level discussions about which strategy to use, to detailed analyzes of how subtle shifts in modeling or scaffolding lead to different results.

When teachers have a sustained opportunity to collaborate in addressing a student outcome goal until they see tangible results of success, their focus moves from delivery to student learning—and most important—to the cause-and-effect relationship between the two (Gallimore et al., 2009). By focusing on the same goal across multiple lessons in a year, teachers collaborate until they see tangible outcomes of success. It takes more than one or two lessons to address the problems of practice most teams choose, especially when the focus is on academic language learning, equitable participation, and/or literacy. The multilesson cycle helps teams collaborate across student learning progressions, increase rigor, and release responsibility over time. Depending on the complexity of the challenge teams set out to solve, sustaining the same inquiry focus across multiple years, as is common in Japanese Lesson Study (Ermeling & Graff-Ermeling, 2014), is also advantageous.

Long-term focus is advantageous when a goal is yet to be realized and problem is yet-to-be solved. A continuous process of building on student strengths and addressing needs over time is essential to transforming underperformance into achievement.

Multiple Feedback Loops Foster Risk Taking and Innovation

A shift from heavy up-front planning to multiple cycles of testing and refining fosters risk taking and innovation by creating increased opportunities for trial and error. This reflects a culture shift from not just Lesson Study, but from traditional approaches to research and development. It's similar to a shift in how many start-up companies operate when they embrace the lean business model developed by Eric Reis (2011). One aspect of this approach is that entrepreneurs engage in multiple build-measure-learn cycles to test and refine their product. "Lean" principles aren't limited to product development and are also growing in popularity among organizations for social good. The lean approach "encourages testing and experimentation instead of elaborate planning . . . and uses iterative methods over traditional 'big planning up front' development" (Lean Impact, 2014).

Increased Opportunities to Plan From Formative Observation Data

There is wisdom in applying lean principles to collaborative planning, especially when the feedback or student-learning data a team needs to shape their instruction to the precise needs of students is observational data. In the first planning meeting, teachers estimate students' needs based on what individual teachers interpret in their classrooms, but don't yet have a shared experience of gathering observation in a classroom together. This matters especially when a team focuses on ELLs, students of color, or students in poverty, and some teachers begin with low expectations about what students can achieve.

When a team begins with low expectations, the first lesson is built on low expectations. The sooner the team observes a lesson to gather specific data together about what students say and do, the better. Precise formative data helps move conversations beyond "what students can't do" and toward the specific details of the "just right gap" (Heritage, 2007, p. 144) essential for planning effective instruction. Often, the first team-planned lesson is as much about identifying precisely what students can do in relation to a goal as it is about testing an approach. Using the facilitation tools emphasized in this book, multiple iterative cycles of planning-testing-refining based on observational data help teams build from planning on assumptions to planning based on precise insights about where students are and what they need to continue to grow.

With instructional goals such as oral language development, collaborative conversation skills, and critical problem solving, the data teachers need to interpret and understand live in live lessons. Consider the implications of this for collaborating to answer the essential questions for data-driven planning:

1. What are our goals for student learning?

2. What can students now understand and do in relation to those goals?

3. What learning opportunities do we need to provide to help students build from current abilities to realize the goals?

It takes multiple shared experiences of observing students, gathering and analyzing data specific to a goal for a team to develop deep, shared understandings about what success with the goal looks like (#1) and what diverse students can do and understand relative to that goal (#2). This is especially true with oral academic language learning, a complex topic to understand and teach in the context of content teaching. The more opportunities teachers have to collaborate in listening to what students say in academic tasks and analyzing how they use language relevant to those tasks, the better they understand the language demands of their curriculum, where students excel and struggle with those demands, and how to structure content teaching to support deep language learning.

Deepening Learning Across Multiple Contexts

Our brains learn best by making connections. The more connections we make, the more we work with a learned idea across diverse contexts, the deeper our learning. "More connections . . . widen the contexts in which the new understanding may be useful" (Washburn, 2010). In solving a challenge, a team will often choose a theory of action based on research or the recommendation of experts. For example, many teams working to elevate achievement of linguistically diverse learners in reading may focus together on ways to "structure collaborative conversations to deepen reading comprehension." Working to apply, test, and refine the nuances of this concept across multiple lessons helps teachers deepen their capacity to apply the concept in ways that are impossible in a workshop, demonstration lesson, or single Lesson Study. Across five lessons to plan and observe together in a year, there is a new, diverse context each time: a new text with its unique challenges and opportunities. Collaborating in the complex work of applying theory to action across different contexts helps teachers enhance their flexibility and capacity to apply that theory to new situations on their own.

Structured Time to Apply Insights to Individual Teaching

Observing and debriefing a lesson with colleagues is a rich learning experience that leads to understandings about students and pedagogy. Understanding is only the first step, and it only makes a difference when teachers apply it to their individual teaching. The OI process centers on helping teachers collaboratively apply understandings to teaching. The combination of goal setting and time strategically scheduled three- to four-week periods between team meetings supports teachers in applying what they learn to daily teaching. After reflecting on instruction together, teachers have about four weeks to apply their individual goals and test/ refine approaches before meeting with the team again for the next inquiry cycle.

"I like the structure because it gave me a chance to go back into my classroom and practice what had been working, and tweak what hadn't been working." First-grade teacher Joan Boyce reflected. "When we came to generalizations we took what we discussed back to our classrooms, and I think that because we did that we saw a lot of growth with the lessons and the outcomes of the retelling with the kids."

With four team inquiry lessons in a year, teachers have three different segments of time between sessions to apply learning to practice and bring insights back to the team. This is a powerful support for building new instructional habits as teachers set goals, apply them, and reflect together on progress. The space between the team lesson inquiry meetings is as important to the overall learning design as the team meetings themselves.

PROTOCOLS TO FOSTER DEEP COLLABORATION

In any approach to observing live lessons together, the depth of our learning lies in how we talk about what we see. When teams maintain a culture of nice (MacDonald, 2013) and only complement one another after a lesson, they miss an opportunity to learn. On the other hand, when conversations center on critical feedback, there can be a breakdown of the trust essential for collaborative innovation. How we navigate the space between and find the sweet spot for deep, constructive conversations is a primary focus of this book. In Chapters 6 through 8, we'll delve into the details of how to lead deep decisions after an observation with specifics including video examples, protocols, and facilitation tools.

A Structured Approach

In the past decade, I have used different approaches to facilitating conversations, and my approach has evolved over time. I used to facilitate a fairly open conversation that began with the teacher who taught reflecting on the lesson, and then shifted to observer insights, reflections, and constructive critique. In many situations, this worked, but in others I experienced what is also often the case with Lesson Study in the US contexts "teachers and observers maintain politeness at all costs and offer superficial and tentative feedback" (Chokshi & Fernandez, 2004, p. 525). In addressing this challenge, and also working to scale up the approach by building the capacity of multiple teachers to facilitate the process, I integrated a more structured approach to debriefing lessons based in part on the work of City and colleagues with Instructional Rounds (2009).

Observation Inquiry Debrief Protocol

Before a lesson, team members meet briefly to focus the observation on the POP and review priority student evidence to gather during the lesson. After a lesson, teams collaborate to do the following:

1. **Describe.** Write about five specific pieces of student evidence relevant to the POP on self-stick notes and share them without adding interpretation.

2. **Organize.** Collaborate to group data to illuminate trends.

3. **Generalize**. Write generalizations from the data.

4. **Link cause and effect.** Discuss generalizations with specific attention to the cause-and-effect link between instruction and student outcomes. Specify how to replicate successes, and brainstorm ways to address challenges.

5. **Plan.** Build from student data and team learning to plan the next lesson for collaborative observation and analysis.

6. **Set individual and team goals.** Individuals each write a goal to apply to daily teaching before the next meeting. When all share a goal, the team makes an agreement to apply a practice to daily teaching.

The steps of this protocol do more than structure a conversation. They help teams engage together in the following three types of thinking central to analytical and creative problem solving:

Divergent thinking to generate ideas, thinking broadly and creatively to identify possible solutions

Convergent thinking to analyze and synthesize information to draw conclusions from data and prioritize actions

Metacognition to think about their thinking both to support themselves and their students as lifelong learners.

Steps 4 through 6 especially call for the continuous integration of all three types of thinking, a benefit for creative problem solving. According to Bronson and Merryman's (2010) analysis of creativity research, "Genuine creativity requires constant shifting, blender pulses of both divergent thinking and convergent thinking, to combine new information with old and forgotten ideas" (p. 4).

Learning From Instructional Coaching

A central benefit of one-on-one coaching is the opportunity for individuals to set personal goals, work to achieve them, and then reflect on the process. This valuable element of personalized professional learning is not limited to coaching. Within OI, teachers engage in continuous personal goal setting and reflection:

1. At the end of each meeting, each teacher writes a priority goal to apply immediately to daily teaching and shares it with the team.

2. At the start of each meeting, teachers reflect on their implementation of individual goals with the team.

3. The lead teacher teaching a lesson always has the option to share a personal goal and to ask observers to look for evidence specific to that goal.

Goal setting is personal and not limited to the team's collaborative focus. Many relate specifically to the team's POP, and others relate to aspects of instruction such as classroom management. By sharing goals, taking time to work with them between meetings, all participants have continuous opportunities to personalize their professional learning in tandem with the team learning process.

GETTING STARTED

From this point forward, this book is 100% a how-to-guide for applying theory in to practice. While my focus is on how to lead OI, remember that the mindset and facilitation tools can also be applied to other professional learning designs. My dual goal is to share a path and also foster a mindset to continuously question and refine each path you choose according to evidence of impact toward your goals for student and teacher learning.

Logistical Considerations

Leading teams in inquiry begins with logistical questions:

- Who will participate?
- When will they participate?
- Who will cover classes as teachers observe teachers?

This section is about strategies for answering these questions. If you already know who will participate, the times you'll meet and how you'll coordinate coverage for classes during observations, skip to Chapter 3. Otherwise, read on:

Who Participates?

In the ideal world, every team in a school and district has the opportunity to collaborate at the edge of learning in classrooms together. In some schools, all teachers get to engage in classroom-centered professional inquiry.

This is not, however, the only approach. You can begin with one team, a handful of teams or any configuration that is a good match for your goals, resources, and priorities.

Consider these different approaches two districts used to get started and build momentum with OI:

Two Approaches to Getting Started

Plant Seeds Then Grow

Mark West Union School District. Santa Rosa, CA

Mark West Union School District started small. In the first year, site principals shared the vision of OI at their sites and recruited participants for the first district team. One team, including teachers from each of the three sites started the process the first year. In the second year, the district tripled participation by having each year one participant facilitate a site-based team. By the third year, the district maintained the same quantity of participants, but shifted who participated by expanding the focus to include different teachers and grade levels.

The benefits of this approach are that buy-in can be built in baby steps. A district can get started when as few as three to five teachers form a team. People who participate in the first year then share their excitement and bring new colleagues on board.

Begin With 100% Participation

Petaluma City Schools

Under the leadership of curriculum director and assistant superintendent Jane Escobedo, most K–12 schools in the Petaluma City Schools had learning teams in the first year. Several schools started small with volunteers from different grade levels forming one or two teams. At McDowell and McKinley Elementary, however, every grade level, every teacher in the school engaged in OI in the first year.

Involving every team and every teacher is a complex decision as it means the process is not voluntary. Building buy-in and trust in this scenario is especially important, as every teacher must choose to engage for inquiry to be effective. It was a profound shift in the first month, when teachers moved from uncertainty and hesitation to trust and forward momentum with their teams. Once they experienced the safety of the process and benefits of classroom-based collaboration, teams were hooked. Every grade level team voted to continue the same professional learning process the next year.

The benefit of starting schoolwide is that there are increased opportunities for teams to carry their learning into new areas. A fourth-grade team, for example, that engages in four days of classroom-based inquiry in the year can leverage the shared insights from this process to deepen their collaboration in weekly grade-level meetings. At McDowell school, for example, Principal Maureen Rudder reported that even outside the process of learning teams she noticed that teacher teams during their weekly planning time were now having higher-level discussions with an increased emphasis on designing instruction to address student needs.

Choosing Team Configurations

Different team configurations are possible for OI. You may choose to work with teams that already exist (e.g., grade-level or department) or form new teams specifically for this professional learning opportunity. As you plan how to form teams, consider which of the following are your top goals:

- Deepening collaboration in existing teams
- Cross-subject collaboration
- Cross-grade-level articulation
- Bringing expertise from different content areas together to solve a student challenge
- Facilitating deep collaboration between specialists (e.g., ELL) and content teachers

Also determine if participation will be voluntary and how you will recruit, as this shapes team configurations. Will you look for existing teams to sign up as a unit, or individuals to volunteer? When participation depends on individual volunteers, predict the range of teacher roles (e.g., grade level or content area) that may sign up and team configurations that will be possible. Forming teams via individual volunteers typically leads to multigrade, multisubject, or cross-site teams. If job-alike teams are a priority, recruit instead by having existing teams sign up together.

Consider the advantages of each configuration in Figure 2.3.

Use existing teams. Note that some of the team configurations in Figure 2.3 build on teams that exist in a school (e.g., grade-level teams or content area departments). This is always advantageous as the learning team process then becomes a boost for a team that already works together. The insights, shared experiences and protocols they learn via the learning team process will carry over into their ongoing collaboration.

In schools with an effective PLC process in which teams meet to analyze assessment results or student work samples within a cycle of inquiry, it often is beneficial to use the same team configurations for OI. OI and PLC processes complement each other, especially when a PLC focus is not just on determining intervention, but also engaging teachers in cycles of planning, teaching, and reflection to improve instructional needs (Ermeling & Gallimore, 2013). Observation inquiry gives PLCs a process for expanding their ongoing collaboration into classrooms together. The PLC process also enriches OI by engaging teams in weekly collaboration centered on written work and data. In tandem, the two processes are powerful, especially when used to address the same POP.

Figure 2.3   Comparing Team Configurations

Team Configuration	Description	Ideal Context	Advantages
Grade Level	All colleagues on the team teach the same grade level. At an elementary site, this is typically a team that meets for other purposes as well.	Schools where teachers teach multiple subjects and meet regularly in grade-level teams.	Emphasis on one grade allows for specificity and depth of focus on curriculum. The shared experience deepens collaboration for existing grade-level teams.
Subject Area	All colleagues on the team teach the same content area. At a secondary site, this is typically a team that meets for other purposes as well.	Schools where teachers teach single subjects and meet regularly in content area teams.	Emphasis on one subject allows for specificity and depth of focus. The shared experience deepens collaboration for existing content teams.
Multigrade Range	The team includes colleagues from multiple grade levels, such as K–3, 4–8, or 9–12.	Small multisubject schools with one or two teachers per grade level. Any school focused on vertical articulation of learning from one grade to the next.	On a priority focus area, understand and influence the connections from one grade to the next.
Multisubject Range	The team includes teachers of different content areas focused on a common goal.	Schools where teachers teach single subjects and want to collaborate to address a shared priority (e.g., content literacy, EL achievement, critical thinking).	Build on the diverse expertise of team members (content, literacy, ELL) to address a shared cross-content goal.

Create new teams. Even when there are existing teams that meet as PLCs or other collaboration, it can also be valuable to form new teams for OI. Consider creating new teams either within a school or across a district. One drawback of this approach is the collaboration only continues during the structured OI time. That said, there are several advantages to creating new teams for OI including the following:

- Bringing diverse expertise together (e.g., literacy experts and content teachers)

- Addressing a priority that crosses grade-level or content areas
- Building teams based on volunteers

When Will Teams Participate?

Plan a minimum of one full day to launch the process, using the agenda in Appendix A. After this initial workshop, plan four three-hour blocks, scheduled one month a part through the year. An alternative to three-hour blocks is to schedule lesson release times in tandem with afterschool meetings, as detailed in the next section on covering classes.

Sample Schedule

August or September	October	November/ December	January	February
Launch the Process	Inquiry Cycle 1	Inquiry Cycle 2	Inquiry Cycle 3	Inquiry Cycle 4
Six to nine hours during nonstudent time, or release time to build trust, train in protocols, choose a focus and plan	Three to four hours including a 30- to 45-minute lesson that every team member observes	Three to four hours including a 30- to 45-minute lesson that every team member observes	Three to four hours including a 30- to 45-minute lesson that every team member observes	Three to four hours including a 30- to 45-minute lesson that every team member observes

Who Covers Classes?

Most districts opt to book half-day subs for each inquiry cycle day, or roving subs to cover for a morning and afternoon team. For example, at Kawana Academy of Arts and Sciences, teachers book full-day substitute teachers on four inquiry days in the year. From 8:00–11:15 subs cover third and fourth-grade classrooms as teachers meet, from 11:00–2:45 the same subs cover fifth- and sixth-grade classrooms as teachers meet. Within a half-day block, the teams follow this agenda:

- Prelesson meeting (20–25 minutes)
- Lesson to teach/observe (20–40 minutes)
- Debrief, set goals, and plan (120–160 minutes)

Most districts opt to use subs because of ease of scheduling, and teams appreciate the benefit of having prelesson meeting, lesson, and debrief packed into one continuous professional learning activity. On the other hand, some schools prefer not to use subs both to keep costs down and to minimize the time teachers are out of their classrooms.

An alternative without substitute teachers is to have teams meet for the prelesson meeting either at the end of school the previous day or before school that morning. Schedule the lesson debrief at the end of the school day, ideally on a day with an early release schedule. The one time classes need to be covered is for observers during lesson the team observes. Many schools find ways to release up to four teachers to watch a lesson using one or more of the following strategies:

- Use a shared prep time, if one exists during student hours.
- Administrator and/or support teacher covers a class.
- Schedule a buddy activity for classes of teachers who are observing. to meet with a higher or lower grade during the lesson observation.

With any of these options, there is a longer time gap between the pre-lesson meeting, lesson, and debrief. Try to minimize this gap by scheduling the lesson on a day the team can also have two hours to meet and debrief after school. If your district has an early release schedule for professional learning on one day of the week, and there is flexibility for teams to use that time, schedule team inquiry on early release days.

If finding time for professional learning is a challenge, I recommend the free workbook Joellen Killion created for Learning Forward titled *Establishing Time for Professional Learning.* Use the following QR code to access it now, or type in the URL listed in the resources at the end of this book:

REFLECTION QUESTIONS

- How is OI similar to professional learning models you have experienced? How is it different?
- Which features of this model are new to you? Which do you want to try?
- What concerns do you have about observing lessons together? What might be holding you back?

3 Opening Doors

Building Buy-In and Trust

One of the greatest successes was getting over the hurdle of teachers not wanting to be observed. They realize now it's not an "I'll getcha" model but a way of collaboratively working together. There's a buzz going around in the district now. Teachers are talking about [observation inquiry] in the lunchrooms . . . the excitement is spreading.

—Kay Schultz, Retired Superintendent,
Mark West Union School District

Once teachers engage in collaborative, observation inquiry (OI) that is relevant and connected to their goals, a momentum builds. They experience the value of collaborating around live lessons to accomplish what no individual teacher could accomplish alone. Tackling complex problems and getting results fuels deeper levels of commitment to continuing the process of planning, teaching, observing, and refining instruction as a team.

It doesn't start this way. In fact, it often begins with a statement such as, "Our teachers are not open to having peers in their classrooms." This was Superintendent Kay Schultz's first response when I approached her with the idea of beginning OI in Mark West schools. The challenge she identified in her district is universal and a product of the history and structure of teacher isolation in US schools. Even factoring in peer coaching opportunities, the majority of US teachers rarely, if ever, see one another teach (Wei, Darling-Hammond, Andree, Richardson, & Orphanos, 2009). In many schools, there is a culture of privacy where an unspoken expectation reigns: We respect one another best by leaving the teaching to the individual, behind closed doors.

Reluctance to peer observation is compounded by the fact that the primary contexts for lesson observation in schools involve a hierarchy of roles. Principals observe teachers to evaluate their performance. Teachers observe a coach, or are observed by a coach, to learn from the coach's expertise. When these scenarios are the only frames of reference for observations, colleagues on equal standing are hesitant to begin any initiative that involves watching one another teach. Hesitation grows to resistance when we factor in the ubiquitous truth: Most of us are nervous about having colleagues watch us teach.

Opening Doors

Inspiring teachers to open their classroom doors is the most important task in initiating OI. It is also the most challenging. Changing an unspoken culture of privacy and moving people to take risks teaching and observing together requires visionary leadership. Such leadership doesn't require authority of position, but can be about influence—the ability to bring people together around a shared vision and inspire action. Whether you are an administrator, consultant, coach, or teacher, you can be the catalyst for change.

The first key is to be optimistic. Hold the vision of what is possible and recognize that the status quo is not a roadblock to change, but an opportunity. When looking honestly at a closed-door culture and listening to people's resistance to being observed, it can be easy to conclude that this won't work at your school. Accepting challenges as barriers is one of the top reasons change initiatives fail (Kotter, 2012). To lead growth, we must believe in what is possible before it exists. When people say it can't be done, listen to their reasons. Ask questions. Look honestly at the challenges, but see them as temporary. Leverage what you know about the difficulties to address them.

Tools for Transformation

The goal of this chapter is to equip readers with a framework of tools for inspiring teachers in a closed-door school to become involved in OI (or any professional learning model involving teachers in classrooms together). Whether you are a teacher hoping to convince a team of colleagues to join you in an ongoing cycle of inquiry or an administrator or consultant working to enhance the collaborative culture of a district or school, these steps will help you build the buy-in and trust required for opening doors:

1. Inspire action

2. Honor fears

3. Establish safety

4. Foster a growth mindset

5. Address individual needs

Activities in this chapter focus on the context of building schoolwide change in meetings involving teachers from multiple teams. See Appendix A for how these activities build into a comprehensive sequence of professional learning to lead a culture shift in a school or district. A schoolwide approach is one way to begin the process of building buy-in and trust. As you read, consider also ways you might use the same techniques in one-on-one or small group conversations to

- inspire individuals to form a guiding coalition to lead the change;
- build buy-in and trust with potential resisters or leaders, one at a time;
- inspire a team of colleagues to engage in classroom-centered inquiry; and
- inspire voluntary participation from across the district to launch a multischool team.

INSPIRE ACTION

Leading change requires tapping into what motivates people and connecting with both the heart and mind (Goleman, Boyatzis, & McKee, 2002). An explanation of the benefits of OI helps convince the mind. Presenting research-based reasons and logical arguments, as I have done in the first chapters of this book will help many buy in to the idea of planning and observing lessons together. Agreeing with an idea, however, is not the same as changing behavior. Presenting ideas alone will not inspire action, especially when the action requires personal risk and high levels of collaborative trust.

To lead effective change, we must also respect and appeal to people's emotions (Kotter & Cohen, 2012). The truth of this is rooted in human brains: The lymbic brain, a powerful emotional driver, sends impulses to the prefrontal brain, our intellectual center. The prefrontal brain can limit an emotional response ("Don't eat that brownie; you already had one") with what we know as self-control. Self-control can overpower emotional impulses for short-term situations (think New Years' resolutions), but, like a muscle, it tires.

John Haidt (2006) developed a helpful analogy to illustrate how rational thought and emotion interact in our brains. Imagine a small rider sitting atop a six-ton elephant. The rider is the intellect, with reins for control. The elephant is emotion, and follows the directions he gets from the rider, or at least most of the time. If the elephant gets a powerful impulse to go somewhere, however, he goes there no matter what the rider does with the reins.

Leading lasting change requires motivating the elephant (Heath & Heath, 2010). We do this by both tapping into what drives and motivates people and addressing their fears.

Tap Into Universal Motivators

Motivating others begins with listening. To lead change at a school site, take time in daily conversations to understand the teachers' values and aspirations. Why do they teach? What do they love in their work? What haunts them about it? What do they want to do better each year? The more you understand about people in a school, the more effectively you can motivate collective change.

Daily, one-on-one conversations are powerful, yet they are not always easy to pull off in a busy school setting. They are a great option for colleagues who interact daily, and are also tough to schedule for those leading from outside a school site, such as a consultant or district-level leader. Learn what you can through daily interactions, and also structure focused opportunities to listen.

Illuminating Universal Motivators (10 minutes)

This is a warm-up activity I recommend for a first meeting with teachers, or a meeting in which the agenda involves introducing an idea that challenges the status quo.

1. Acknowledge that teaching is a tough job.

2. Ask, "What inspires you to teach? Share one memory of an experience in the classroom, or a vision you have, that inspires you to return to the classroom again and again."

3. Have teachers answer the question first with partners, then share with the group.

4. As teachers talk, write key phrases and ideas on chart paper.

5. Read the list collectively, identifying universals that emerge.

As people talk about what inspires them, positive energy builds in the room. In diverse groups of educators across diverse schools, universal themes emerge. Educators thrive on the "aha" moments when a kid who struggled finally gets it. We feel overwhelmed when there are too many details to juggle and what matters most slips through the cracks. We want to feel supported with resources and tools that help us do our jobs well. We want to make a difference for kids.

Tap into these universal motivators and use the words, phrases, and ideas teachers share in this conversation when you articulate a vision for bringing teacher teams into classrooms together.

Leverage Shared Challenges

When teams identify a shared challenge, the focus of the next chapter, they identify questions that matter and a problem to solve. Using student data, they get specific together about an area in which they want to see growth and set a student-learning goal that serves as a shared vision for change. The power of this activity extends beyond the benefits of data-driven decision making; it builds a compelling reason for change (Kotter, 2012). When teachers identify a problem of practice (POP) that matters to them, especially one that has been difficult to address alone, they create a shared purpose for opening their doors together for deep collaborative work.

It works well to begin the initial process of identifying a shared POP, before introducing the idea of observing lessons together. Then, as you introduce a vision for OI, be specific with examples from the challenge areas each team identified. For example, in one primary school with a high population of English learners, the kindergarten and first-grade teachers identified oral language and participation as a major challenge area. Teachers struggled to engage students in talking about academic topics, or participating verbally at all. When building a vision, I referenced the team's specific goal: "Wouldn't it be powerful to collaborate together on that difficult challenge of engaging all English learners in dynamic conversations? Imagine having an opportunity to collaborate in planning a lesson, observe what students say and do together, and then refine the approach together based on what you see."

Whatever challenges the teams in your school identify, emphasize the moment in the classroom that an individual teacher faces the challenge, and then share the vision of what that same moment will look like when a team tries strategies together, watches students, and refines the best approach to get the desired results. By building on the precise goals teams set from their data, you are already speaking about a vision that matters. It's not *your* goal, but teachers' tangible, relevant, student-learning goal that builds from their frustrations and hopes. This builds an emotional connection to the rationale for collaborating in new ways.

Build From Success

Sharing testimonials of teachers who have participated in OI also builds interest in the process. At the end of each cycle of inquiry, plan to solicit honest feedback from all participants. This not only helps you reflect and refine your approach, but also often leads to quotes that are inspiring for teachers new to the process. Seek permission to share these quotes.

One way to share testimonials is to project or print quotes for teachers to read, and then provide time for reflection. Have teachers identify a phrase or line that resonates with their interests and needs. It is most powerful to share testimonials from known teachers within a district, but even quotes from other districts, such as the following, can motivate action:

> *"This process has been empowering, motivating and reinspiring. It is morale boosting. It makes us more of a team, and . . . reignites my passion for teaching."*
>
> Lisa Ryan, Third-Grade Teacher
>
> *"It is a helpful process because it's nonthreatening, inviting teachers to collaborate to address a student challenge, and move forward as a team. This is how we should be spending our professional development time: utilizing all the knowledge we have right on campus."*
>
> Brigitta Hunter, Fourth-Grade Teacher
>
> *"[I appreciated] being able to work together as a group and not as four separate teachers in our four separate kingdoms. [Observation inquiry] has made the whole year more effective, and more fun."*
>
> Shannon Bourdage, Seventh-Grade Teacher

Use this QR code to access more inspiration: a 45-second video of teachers reflecting on OI with colleagues:

Notice that the quotes speak to something most of us crave: meaningful, motivating work. They speak to a vision for collaborative professional learning that is purposeful and inspiring.

HONOR FEARS

After inspiring initial interest in the concept of OI, introduce the model to help teachers visualize the process and what it means for them in time and participation. The OI overview in Chapter 2 is a good tool for this initial introduction. Explain the steps of the cycle, and expect that the first time you introduce the "teach and observe" part of the cycle, and share the value of having every team member teach a lesson, anxiety will increase in the room.

Even if people are smiling and nodding, imagine that at least one teacher is having an internal "aha" realization akin to, "Wait a minute! This means I have to teach when my peers are watching. Forget it! I'm not signing up for that!" This is the moment when the rational brain (the rider with the reins) agrees with the concept in the abstract, but gets overpowered by the emotional response: fear. Even the elephant inspired by a compelling vision to follow the rider will run in the opposite direction if afraid.

Expect fear, and address it. Share that it is natural to feel anxiety about having colleagues in our rooms as we teach. Assure teachers that they will feel more comfortable once they experience the nonjudgmental protocols for discussing lessons together, but don't say more than these brief statements. Rational reasons will not convince the elephant. Instead of trying to control it, take this opportunity to honor its powerful drive.

Brainstorming Fears (25 minutes)

Having teachers brainstorm their worst fears, and then their highest hopes, for the process is a powerful exercise for honoring emotions and focusing this energy in positive ways.

1 Acknowledge that feeling fear about being observed is natural.

2 Ask, "If we begin classroom-based team inquiry and the process turns out to be the worst experience ever, what will happen?"

3 Provide time for teachers to think and write, and then discuss their fears with a colleague.

4 Next, invite volunteers to report ideas to the group, as you write shared fears on chart paper at the front of the room.

5 Don't respond to fears, except to show active listening and honor what people express.

(Activity adapted from Boudett, City, & Russell, 2010.)

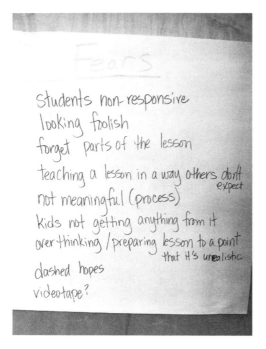

Fears

Students non-responsive
looking foolish
forget parts of the lesson
teaching a lesson in a way others don't expect
not meaningful (process)
kids not getting anything from it
over thinking / preparing lesson to a point that it's unrealistic
dashed hopes
videotape?

Transforming fears into a tangible list validates individuals and illuminates universal emotions. This is a unifying experience, and most fears expressed elicit immediate nods and agreement. Across diverse school districts with very different teacher populations and staff cultures, this activity consistently elicits similar themes and global fears.

Fears frequently shared in teams include the following:

- The lesson doesn't work out the way I hope.
- Kids act out when observers are there.
- I'm uncomfortable with having observers in my room.
- It is a waste of time.
- There is no growth for the students.
- There is no improvement in my teaching.

What themes do you notice in these fears?

The first three fears center around the universal fear of judgment, which is the most important fear to address when establishing and maintaining safety and trust. The next three center on a universal desire to have our actions matter. In our time-crunched profession, educators are justifiably selective of any approach for professional learning. We can't afford to waste time. We need our actions to yield results. Notice the shared vision that lies in the inverse of these fears: We want to use our time powerfully, we want to see changes in student learning, and we want to become stronger as teachers. Each of these fears can be a powerful motivator when we see it also in its inverse form—as a vision for forward momentum: hope.

Illuminate Hopes: A Shared Vision for Change

After brainstorming and acknowledging fears, shift from the "worst-possible" to "best-possible" scenario and elicit hopes. Ask teachers to imagine that their participation in action teams yields the best professional learning opportunity of their career. Initiate a brainstorm of hopes for what participation in the process could achieve.

In the following list of hopes that one school of teachers brainstormed together, notice how many speak to a vision for learning and growth:

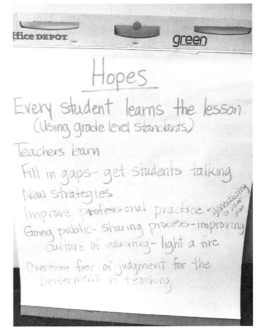

- We see best practices in action.
- We learn a data-driven, collaborative process we can continue to use.
- We increase student achievement.
- We increase motivation and engagement for teachers and students.
- We become increasingly comfortable adjusting instruction to meet student needs.
- The cycle benefits more than our inquiry focus and is transferrable to other areas of the curriculum.
- We share a common experience and build a common language.
- We develop a consistent use of effective strategies.

The hopes in this list are expressed time and again by teachers. These also tap into what best-selling author Daniel Pink (2009) argues are two of the principal motivators for productive work: the drives for mastery and for purpose. Brainstorming hopes illuminates teachers' shared drive to make a difference, and often a vision for change. People are most invested in a vision that builds on their values and aspirations (Kouzes & Posner, 2009). This collaboratively generated list of hopes is more powerful for building buy-in than any bullet points a leader can provide, as the visionary outcomes are articulated through teachers' hopes and in their words.

ESTABLISH SAFETY

I learned the most from taking the risk of teaching in front of colleagues, from trying new things in a safe environment.

Katie Cervone, Fifth-Grade Teacher, Mark West School

Any professional learning design that involves colleagues seeing one another teach requires high-levels of emotional safety and trust. Teachers need to feel comfortable and be assured that this is not an evaluative process, but a safe opportunity to take risks and grow.

Establish Team Norms

Norms are collaboratively written agreements explaining how all members of a team will act and behave to ensure trust, safety, and productivity through the yearlong inquiry process. Examples of norms include

- arrive on time, ready to begin;
- accept diverse opinions;
- refrain from side conversations when observing lessons;
- maintain confidentiality: What is shared in our team stays with our team;
- encourage risk taking over perfection; and
- contribute to all discussions.

Guide Teams in Writing Norms (20 minutes)

It is valuable for teams to write norms together.

You may lead this activity within a team or with multiple teams in a room each working at their own table with chart paper and markers.

1. Post the previously brainstormed list(s) of fears and hopes.

2. Explain the purpose of norms and provide examples.

3. Give teams the open-ended task of creating and writing norms.

4. When multiple teams are in the room, conclude with a gallery walk, in which each team posts norms, has time to read posted norms, and then returns to their list to collaboratively reflect and refine.

Norms only matter if all are accountable to follow them. Accountability can be tricky, as often when someone violates a norm, colleagues usually feel uncomfortable speaking up. Professional learning community expert Kenneth Williams recommends that teams prepare for this in advance by asking immediately after creating norms, "What happens when someone violates a norm? How are we going to hold each other accountable in a respectful and dignified manner?" (Armstrong, 2014).

The solution may be as simple as a silent signal any can use to efficiently, respectfully remind a colleague to follow the norms.

Plan to revisit norms in each meeting by posting norms, reading them together and/or taking time to reflect together on norms in the last minutes of each meeting. For additional structure, create a norms "job" that rotates. The person's role is to validate use of norms, provide norm reminders as needed, and facilitate a reflection on norms at the end of each meeting.

Establish Collective Responsibility

Establishing collective responsibility deepens trust within teams preparing to teach and observe lessons together. Collective responsibility means all team members share accountability for the work and outcomes of the team. At the core of collective responsibility is the feeling that "we are in this together"—equal participants working to meet shared goals—a feeling that is of critical importance when asking teachers to open their classroom doors for peer observation. Compare, for example, these two scenarios:

A. You and your team plan four lessons that you watch together. Over the course of a year, every team member teaches one of the lessons as colleagues watch. When it is your turn to teach, you know that every observer in the room has also been, or will be, in your shoes.

B. You and your team meet to plan every lesson you observe and discuss together. Half of the team members offer little input during the planning process, and choose not to teach any of the team lessons in the year. When you teach, they happily take notes and discuss the lesson, but won't open their doors to switch roles.

In which scenario would you feel more comfortable teaching? Which will encourage more risk-taking behavior during instruction? Which is more likely to fuel a team culture of mutual trust?

Scenario A, with the shared expectation that everyone on a team will teach one of the observed lessons, consistently yields the strongest sense of mutual accountability and trust. It is the tougher structure to begin, however, as it requires every teacher to buy in to the idea of opening classroom doors. The payoff is worth it as having every teacher teach a team lesson fosters interdependence, mutual trust, and a shared investment in adhering to norms and protocols that ensure safety.

Collective responsibility extends beyond sharing in the role of teaching lessons. Team members also share responsibility through all stages of the OI process, including the following:

- Data analysis, planning, observation, reflection, and problem solving
- Continuous goal setting and application of learning to classroom practice
- Using shared assessments to measure impact

At the early stages of establishing safety and trust, share the global vision of collective responsibility. Establish the premise that participants will share all aspects of team inquiry including the teaching of lessons with colleagues in the room.

Use a Protocol for Observing and Debriefing Lessons

Clear protocols for observation and debriefing help ensure that every postlesson conversation fuels both team trust and ongoing inquiry to advance student learning. Chapters 6, 7, and 8 prepare readers to effectively facilitate using protocols that help teams delve deeply into lesson data while ensuring safety and trust. When establishing safety for new teams, use the resources and video tools in these chapters to introduce and practice all aspects of the debriefing process. Anxiety about observations always lowers when teachers understand what observers will be focused on, and how the team will discuss what they see.

Teach and Practice Nonevaluation

Before immersing new teams in an inquiry cycle, preteach the first step of the debrief process: describing without judgment. Teaching this step early has an added benefit: It helps teachers see and feel exactly how the protocol creates safety by removing judgment from the conversation and focusing on students and what they say and do as evidence of learning.

See Chapter 6 for detailed professional learning activities to engage teams in observing and describing details in a lesson without evaluation. With practice, teachers internalize the norm and make it a game to notice judgments whenever they arise, even in casual conversations outside the team inquiry process. This shared awareness builds safety. When teams learn together to describe without judgment and hold one another accountable for doing the same, they experience deeper feelings of collaborative trust and increased comfort opening classroom doors.

FOSTER A GROWTH MINDSET

The reason to avoid judgment when describing what we see in classrooms together is not simply to protect teachers' feelings. It is a research-based approach to fostering a growth mindset for the team and an essential mindset for deep collaborative learning. Avoiding judgment narrows the focus to concrete evidence of student learning while also steering people away from making praise statements such as, "You are such a good teacher," or, "You are amazing!" According to psychologist Carol Dweck (2008), such praise actually hinders learning by fostering a fixed mindset: the perspective that talent and intelligence are unchangeable.

A fixed mindset leads to a focus on using experiences to evaluate talent rather than develop it. In teaching, this translates to the belief that there are "good teachers" and "bad teachers," and no matter what a teacher does, his or her ability to teach stays about the same. When we have a fixed mindset, we interpret a classroom success as evidence that we are a talented teacher, and a struggle as evidence that we are not. With this mindset, the idea of having anyone observe us is terrifying. We think that any success or mistake defines the kind of teacher we are. So we play it safe and avoid risks to maintain our identity as a good teacher.

In contrast, when we have a growth mindset, we believe that abilities can be developed by effort and work. We know that what we are able to do is not fixed, but changeable. By taking risks and learning from challenges, we can develop our talent and intelligence in new ways. Teams thrive with a growth mindset. Because they aren't thinking about rating teacher talent, they don't fear risks. When a growth-oriented team observes a challenge in the classroom, they leverage it to gain insights into where students struggle and what specifically they need.

Focus on Effort, not Talent

In her extensive research on mindsets, Dweck (2008) studied the factors that lead a learner to avoid or embrace challenges. In a key study of fifth graders, Dweck had female research assistants invite one student at a time at a time to participate in a "test" of solving puzzles that were easy enough for all of the students. In randomly selected groups, half were praised for intelligence (e.g., "You must be smart at this!"), while half were praised for effort (e.g. "You must have worked really hard"). After students finished the first group of puzzles, they were given two options for a second test: one that would be more difficult, or one that would be easier.

Among the students who were praised for effort, 90% chose the harder puzzles. By contrast, the majority of those who received evaluative praise

for intelligence chose the easier test. Consider these results and their impli-
cation for adult learning in collaborative teams. When we want teachers to
have high expectations of all students and embrace the challenges of
addressing diverse student needs, we must avoid evaluative praise. A
focus on the effort will yield more powerful results.

After watching a colleague teach a lesson, it is natural to feel the
social impulse to say, "Good job!" Prepare teams with an alternative that
doesn't involve a judging adjective. Say, for example, "Thank you for
opening your classroom to our team," or "Thank you for your risk taking
and hard work."

Value Imperfection

To foster a growth mindset in teams, value, model, and encourage
imperfection in the lessons the team builds and tests together. Trial and
error is at the core of learning. When babies learn to talk, they babble
before forming words. When toddlers learn to walk, they stumble and fall
in the process of getting it right. Any new learning requires that we reach
from what we know to attempt something new. The moment of reaching
is open ended and imperfect. The star basketball player pushing his talents
misses shots. The concert pianist practicing new approaches hits a wrong
note. Mistakes happen again and again when we stretch our limits and
refine our skills.

Yet typically, when teachers teach with an observer in the room, especially if the observer is a principal, they feel a pressure to avoid risks and
play it safe. As one teacher told me frankly, "You can't afford to bomb
when an administrator observes you. You need to be a superstar." During
planned, formal observations, most teachers feel pressure to shine in an
area of confidence rather than fumble around with something beyond
their grasp. Observations in OI, however, should inspire the opposite.
Planning, teaching, and debriefing an "easy" lesson that teams already
know will be seamless is a waste of precious collaborative time. Instead,
zero in on a challenge no individual has yet been able to solve, and plan
and test a new attempt to solve it together.

Before every lesson, emphasize that the goal is not to teach a perfect
lesson. On the contrary, it is ideal when a lesson doesn't go as planned. I
learned this long before starting OI, when I was a consultant teaching a
"model" lesson in an upper-elementary reading intervention class, a
group of students I was meeting for the first time. At one point in the lesson, students were staring at me in confusion. When I tried to engage them
in partner discussions, with what I expected to be an easy task, they were
silent. I looked from the students to the observers in the back of the room,

and back to the students again. In this brief, but seemingly eternal "sweat it out moment," I changed my plans. In response to the students, I changed the lesson sequence I had printed and shared with teachers before the lesson. Without lowering the bar of my end goal, I adjusted my lesson to connect to the needs of every learner in the room.

In the lesson debrief, the observing teachers commented that they learned the most watching the part of the lesson that didn't go as planned, as it showed them where students struggled, and what they needed to move forward. It also kept our discussion focused on simple how-to strategies for a deeper concept: responsive teaching. Together, we experienced the moment that most teachers usually only experience alone: the moment when we check for understanding and there is none. Witnessing such a moment together deepens the level of discussion and insight in a debrief discussion every single time.

Encourage imperfect think-on-your-feet moments before every team inquiry lesson. Hope to experience one when you teach with teachers observing in the room. Moments that illuminate student challenges or the impact of adjusting instruction on the spot are a gift to team learning.

Model Risk Taking

A surefire way to model risk taking is to teach the first lesson teams observe, especially when you approach the lesson as a lifelong learner who embraces challenges along the way. Don't try to teach a perfect lesson. Within the context of the team-planned lesson, identify something you are going to test out, to advance your learning as a teacher. Share your questions and uncertainty with the team. For example, in a team lesson taught by a team facilitator and involving pair-share, the facilitator told observers,

> "Often when I structure pair-share, I keep interactions short because I fear students will get off-task. Yet I've noticed that students rarely extend conversations beyond each person saying a sentence. I'm going to push my comfort edge a little today and provide more time to encourage the back-and-forth discussions we want to see. I don't know how it will work, and am glad you will be with me in the room gathering data about what students say and do."

Notice the curiosity and uncertainty in this statement—feelings that are a normal part of taking on a challenge. If she hadn't said anything, and the pair-share discussions worked well, observers would likely infer there was no trial and error involved. To inspire risk taking and growth, leaders need to be vulnerable. Leaders initiating and facilitating teams need to be open about how they are learners, too.

Be Sincere About Fear

For teachers still warming up to the idea of being observed by a team, it also helpful to watch someone move from initial jitters to teaching in front of others. If you feel even slightly nervous before you teach a lesson in front of teams, be sincere about your fear. Sharing vulnerability may seem tough, especially if you have a leadership role in a school, but remember the goal of the first lesson is not to prove expertise, but to lead teams into growth-focused work.

Even though I have been teaching lessons in other teachers' classrooms professionally for years, my nerves race and my heart rate speeds up every time I prepare to do it again. Rather than hiding my internal process to present myself as the fearless consultant, I share my experience right before the lesson, to honor the fear I expect others to feel at this point. "My heart is racing," I say. "I always feel nervous energy before teaching a lesson with others in the room." I take a few breaths, and then share a strategy I use to calm my nerves. Calming strategies and reminders include the following:

- Take deep breaths.
- Focus on the students and how to make them comfortable.
- Remember that imperfections and the unexpected are a gift to team inquiry.

Anxiety about being observed drops considerably for most teachers the moment we begin to teach. Once we meet the challenge of stepping into the room with a team of observers, the teaching is the easy part. Out of necessity, our focus shifts immediately to the students before us. Instead of thinking about ego (where fixed-mindset performance anxiety resides), we become engrossed in the task at hand. The lesson has been planned, and we get to be in the moment teaching something we believe is important, to help kids learn in new ways.

> "I could see how it could be nerve racking, but you know, once you get into it . . . your focus is the goal that you are trying to achieve for these students. That's your focus. And you start to realize . . . it's not me on stage. It's 'What can we do to benefit these kids?'"
>
> Jenifer Rush, Team Facilitator,
> San Miguel Elementary School

Courage is not the absence of fear, but the ability to move through it. When we take the lead in this arena and demonstrate the safety guaranteed through our mindset, the debrief protocols, and established norms, others gain the confidence to follow.

ADDRESS INDIVIDUAL NEEDS

When teachers understand and feel the value and safety of bringing collaboration into the classroom, they become motivated to open doors and get involved. Across diverse schools and districts, I have found the recommendations in this chapter are enough to inspire a shift for the majority of teachers. Majority is the keyword here.

A deep, collaborative process involving risk taking and trust works best when participation is voluntary. That said, there are ways to inspire participation across an entire team or school, even when there are individuals who are reluctant to participate.

When working to shift the culture of privacy in a team or school and engage everyone in opening doors to teaching/observing together, leaders need to find personalized ways to connect to the minority of teachers who hesitate to get involved. In two different schools focused on engaging all teachers, the reluctant minority was one individual teacher. In each case, the teacher was willing to be part of a team, but not open to teaching a team-observed lesson. In these situations, a top-down mandate generally would make the situation worse. I prefer to set high expectations and then support individuals in making a choice that works for them and the team.

An effective strategy is for the principal and team facilitator to (1) set the expectation for participation, (2) follow all the steps outlined in this chapter, and (3) meet one on one with any individuals who still have concerns. The following recommendations are critical to the success of these one-on-one conversations:

- Listen first to understand (Covey, 2004). Be a reflective listener.
- Assure that you will not force the individual to teach in front of colleagues.
- Stress why you hope the individual will choose to teach in front of colleagues:

  o It helps build team trust when everyone opens classroom doors.
  o It is a valuable learning experience.

- Collaborate to find a solution that will work for the teacher and for the team.

The best solution will vary by teacher and situation. In one school, a teacher was wrestling with severe anxiety, and was concerned about the increase in adrenaline teaching in front of peers would create. I listened empathetically, and we brainstormed together how to honor her needs and also ensure safety for her team. She shared her situation with her team, and asked if they would feel comfortable letting her wait to commit to teaching one of the team lessons. The team agreed. She did not teach the last lesson, but participated as an active team member all year.

In another scenario, a teacher resisted and went to the union to protest. When I listened to her concerns and assured her it was ultimately her choice whether to teach a lesson with colleagues in the room, she became more open to the idea. In this case, a focus on teacher ownership enabled us to shift the energy from power struggle to possibility. She agreed to be on the team, and to be the last one to teach a lesson. Over the course of the year, she became an active participant in every inquiry cycle, and surprised her team by volunteering to facilitate the OI process. With a sense of ownership, she became a leader both in team meetings and by opening her classroom doors. When she taught a team lesson, she raised the bar for the entire team by demonstrating with her students a level of student discourse not yet seen in previous lessons. If she'd been let too easily off the hook in the beginning, or shutdown through a mandate-inspired power struggle, her team would have missed the value of her contributions.

As you begin the process of building buy-in and trust, remember that initial resistance and fear is natural. If individuals resist, listen and respect their perspective. You may be surprised by the outcome. The most powerful initial resisters may become the strongest leaders and advocates for OI.

REFLECTION QUESTIONS

- How do you feel about teaching with colleagues in the room? How do teachers in your setting feel about teaching in front of others?
- Will you recruit eager volunteers or lead a culture shift to engage an entire team, school, or district in OI? What are possible challenges to this approach, and how will you address them?
- How will you inspire participation and build trust to get started?

4 Asking Questions That Matter

"Questions are more relevant than answers. Questions are bigger than answers. One good question can give rise to several layers of answers, can inspire decades-long searches for solutions, can generate whole new fields of inquiry, and can prompt changes in entrenched thinking. Answers, on the other hand, often end the process."

—Stuart Firestein (2012, p. 11).

When leading professional learning, we often feel a need to be experts. The irony of this is that expert is a noun. It doesn't move. Leading learning requires a verb. We must be learners. We must know how to push the edge of what we *don't* know: be uncertain, ask questions to which we don't have answers, and be resourceful to pursue new knowledge. As learning leaders, we must model the courage of stepping from the comfort zone of what we do well to explore what we have not mastered. This is how we lead learning and inspire teachers to transform their practice in new ways.

Professional learning, without this edge, is a series of activities that don't change what people think or do. Imagine the unfortunately familiar scenario: Teachers gather in a team to look at data and discuss instruction, then return to their classrooms to teach in exactly same ways as they did before. This scenario repeats easily when teams keep the focus of their conversations and collective work within the comfort zone of what they already know.

To make professional learning powerful, we must lead our colleagues and ourselves to and beyond the edge of what we know and can do. This chapter is about the first step in finding that edge: identifying a focus for observation inquiry (OI), a focus involving questions for which we don't have all the answers and challenges that matter so much to teachers that they are willing to take risks to solve them.

IDENTIFYING A PROBLEM TO SOLVE

Teams begin OI by identifying a focus to drive their collaborative work. They write their focus as a problem of practice (POP) or challenge to address. The POP should be so important that solving it will make a significant difference for student achievement. An ideal POP focuses on factors within a schools' control to change, especially the instructional core: teacher, student, content (City, Elmore, Fiarman, & Teitel, 2009). In schools striving to close opportunity gaps, there are often many possible problems of practice to choose from. The goal of the next section of this chapter is to help teams narrow down the choices and prioritize one focus that will have a significant impact on their learning and the learning of their students. An ideal POP for OI involves a synthesis of three key factors:

1. Alignment with school/district initiatives

2. An opportunity for student learning

3. An opportunity for teacher learning

Problem of Practice Examples

Literacy

Students often demonstrate literal comprehension in reading assessments and classroom discussions but struggle to make inferences and support their thinking with textual evidence. Many only retell literal details in speaking and writing tasks that require critical analysis of texts.

Math

Problem solving is especially challenging for our underperforming students. They often don't seem to understand what is being asked, but instead, they choose numbers from the problem and try an operation to solve it quickly. When asked to justify their answers, many point at the algorithm they solved. They struggle to analyze and discuss the problem with precision.

Science

Students make predictions and observations easily, yet struggle with analyzing and interpreting data to draw conclusions. Their greatest challenge is with tasks requiring analyzing numerical data to identify patterns and trends.

Cross-Disciplinary ELL Focus

When asked open-ended questions that elicit high-level thinking, many of our long-term English learners struggle to respond. Some take a passive role in classroom discussions. Others participate but express their ideas using short sentences. Teachers find it challenging to integrate high-level discussions into daily lesson plans and to manage those discussions so all participate deeply.

Student Subgroup Focus

A high percentage of students receiving free or reduced lunch are underperforming in reading comprehension relative to their peers. As teachers, we want to know more about how students in this subgroup who are struggling in reading engage with texts and how to shift instruction to collectively meet their needs.

21st-Century Focus

Students have limited opportunities to develop 21st-century learning goals of creativity and collaboration. Teachers ask, "How can we embed creative thinking tasks into our instruction to enhance, rather than distract from, content learning?"

Notice that these POP statements specify a problem to solve in the present tense, rather than a goal in the future tense. This subtle difference in wording helps ground teams in the realities of the present before focusing forward on solutions. The content and format of these examples also illustrate the many possible variations in how teams might write a POP. Some include challenges for students and others focus on challenges for teachers. Some are all statements, and others include questions. More important than format is the emphasis and how relevant it is for the team. Does it align with local initiatives? Does it pinpoint an opportunity for student learning? Does it emphasize an area in which teachers want to further develop their expertise?

ALIGNING WITH LOCAL INITIATIVES

As you can see in the examples previously, a POP can be written about *any* challenge a team identifies as important to student learning. The options are limitless. Limitless can be wonderful or overwhelming. As facilitators, we make this process most powerful when we choose a context to narrow the focus, a context aligned to top school/district priorities and learning initiatives already under way.

Aligned and connected are critically important qualities in professional learning design (Wei, Darling-Hammond, Andree, Richardson, & Orphanos, 2009). When beginning OI, make sure it is not "one more thing" to add on top of teachers' work in schools. It is not a new focus, but a *process* for achieving success with a focus that is already on the forefront of educators' minds. A professional learning design is never a destination in itself, but a path for addressing the student learning priorities that matter most to students, teachers, and schools.

Connection is essential because it

- builds buy-in;
- supports deep learning;
- facilitates follow-through; and
- prevents overwhelm and burnout.

Umbrella Goal

Plan alignment to district initiatives by identifying an umbrella context for team inquiry. An umbrella context narrows the options by providing a "big idea" goal within which teams choose their POP focus. It is ideally meets the following criteria:

- A data-driven priority for advancing student learning
- A priority for advancing teacher learning
- Broad enough to allow teams flexibility in using student data to choose a POP that matters
- Narrow enough to connect team inquiry to school or district initiatives

For example, one district focused on raising ELL achievement in literacy made this goal the umbrella context for team inquiry. District leaders choose this focus based on data of low ELL achievement in literacy and a priority to build teacher expertise in addressing this complex challenge. The goal is broad enough teams have flexibility in choosing a more specific POP relevant to their grade-level or subject area goals, student data and priorities for student learning. It's narrow enough align the work of all teams to the district focus on literacy achievement.

Another district emphasizing a shift to 21st-century learning might set an umbrella goal to create opportunities for all students to think critically and creatively around core lesson content. This is another example of goal that is broad enough to allow flexibility and yet specific enough to align the work of teams with the district focus on having students "think critically and creatively." Notice the similarities and differences in these two examples.

Umbrella Goal	Data That Illuminates This as a Priority	Content Area	Student Subgroup
Raise ELL achievement in literacy	State and local ELA assessments	Language arts and content literacy	English learners
Increase opportunities for students to think critically and creatively around core lesson content	Gap analysis of current curriculum compared to 21st-century career expectations	Any	Any

As these two examples illustrate, there is a range in the types of umbrella goals a school or district might set. Our data-driven priority could come from an analysis of pencil-to-paper assessments, observations, or even a gap analysis between current realities and a vision for a different educational paradigm. It can narrow the focus of our efforts to one content area or cut across all. It narrows the focus to one group of students or emphasizes all. What matters is that the umbrella goal comes directly from a shared vision, initiative, and momentum in your district or school. It fits in a systematic framework for aligned professional learning across the organization. It is a goal that matters and has the potential to transform teaching and learning.

If you are in a school or district engaged in a clearly focused initiative for advancing student learning, choosing an umbrella context is as easy as stating the student learning outcome goal of that initiative. You know your priority focus. Write it down, use it to frame OI, and skip the next section.

Narrow the Focus

This section is for the rest of us. Many districts share a problem I know too well in my personal life: juggling too many goals and initiatives. We are ambitious, especially when we care deeply about equity and excellence in education. We want to address every student-learning challenge now. And we work in a field with layers of ambitious decision making at teacher, team, site, district, state, and national levels. In education, change initiatives procreate like spring bunnies. Even when we set priorities, new ones continuously leap into view.

Let's take a moment to brainstorm those priorities, both the ones we choose and the ones hopping before us. Then we'll hone in to choose an umbrella goal that will be the most powerful context for OI.

Identify the Focused Umbrella Goal

Purpose: This activity helps learning leaders identify clearly how OI will align to local initiatives by writing an umbrella goal to frame the context for team inquiry. This is primarily designed to help leaders set the stage for OI across multiple teams, and it can also help the facilitator of one team identify alignment.

Directions: Brainstorm answers to the following questions. First, write the first ideas that come to mind when you answer each question. Every answer is valid in a brainstorm so include even wild ideas on the page. Don't edit or cross out yet.

If you are leading professional development within a team or school, answer for the school. If across a district, answer for the district.

1. *Student learning.* What are our top priorities for advancing student learning for *every* student?

   a. Answer based on intuition

   b. Answer based on student data

   c. Answer based on hard-to-quantify goals (e.g., student initiative, collaboration, engagement, high-level thinking, etc.).

   d. If you have not identified subgroups in the previous answers ask these questions: Are there groups of students who are underperforming relative to their peers? Are there specific subgroups that are a top priority to address as we work to meet the needs of every child?

2. *Teacher learning.* Now aim to narrow the focus by considering the same list from a new frame of reference: teacher learning. Review the list of student learning priorities and ask: Of these goals, which provide the best opportunity for teachers to deepen expertise and advance instructional practice? With some challenges, for example, teachers already

understand what to do to realize a solution. Others challenges have educators throwing arms in the air asking, "How?" Put a star next to the goals with the best opportunities to deepen teacher expertise and shift instruction.

3. *Consider big picture influences.* Zoom out your frame of reference one more time to brainstorm a list of current or recent change influences on instruction across a site or district. Consider the following:

   • Professional learning workshops in the last few years
   • New adoptions of curriculum or technology
   • Shifts in standards or assessments
   • Shifts in teacher evaluation or what administrators prioritize to look for in classrooms

Ask if any of these influences are creating a strong demand for professional learning support? For example, when many states shifted to Common Core State Standards, learning the new standards and assessments rose to the top of the professional learning priority list in most districts. A district level change, such as a new kindergarten through sixth-grade math curriculum, makes professional learning specific to math instruction a priority focus for kindergarten through sixth-grade teachers.

4. *Prioritize and compare both lists.* The student learning priorities with stars indicating teacher learning priorities and the change influences. Do themes or patterns emerge? Does one content area, student group, or cross-disciplinary goal rise to the top as the priority focus? Are there a few different goals that can be synthesized together into a cohesive whole (e.g., critical thinking, math, common core synthesize to an emphasis on differentiating math instruction to meet the needs of ELs)?

5. *Write an umbrella goal.* Cross-check it to ensure it meets the criteria:

   • Priority for advancing student learning
   • Priority for advancing teacher learning
   • Broad enough to allow teams flexibility
   • Narrow enough to align with school or district initiatives

WRITING A PROBLEM OF PRACTICE

Engaging teams in identifying a POP involves a similar process as the first two steps of identifying an umbrella goal. We integrate intuition and data to set priorities. We build from challenges in student learning to opportunities for shifts in teacher practice.

Writing a Team Problem of Practice

Use this activity to facilitate the process within a team, or in a meeting involving multiple teams each seated together.

1. *Establish purpose.* Imagine collaborating to solve a challenge in student learning that will make a significant difference in students' lives. "Our goal today in each team is to find a shared focus for our collaboration that matters to us and our students." Your team will identify a POP to drive your team's collaborative inquiry this year.

2. *Establish context.* Establish the context and connection to current priorities in the school/district by inviting teams to focus within the context of an umbrella goal, "As you know, a major priority in our school is to elevate the literacy achievement of all students, specifically ELLs and students in poverty." Today, as your team identifies a focus that is directly relevant to your students and curriculum, work within the context of this umbrella goal: advancing literacy for ELLs and students in poverty.

3. *Identify opportunities for student learning.* First brainstorm a list of all ideas, without crossing out or prioritizing. Use teacher reflection and student data to explore these questions, specific to the umbrella goal.

   • What challenges do students now demonstrate in their learning that are critical to address to ensure their success in school and beyond?
   • What does student data show us about what students can now understand and do, and where they struggle to meet grade-level/content/literacy expectations?
   • Are there gaps in how different student groups perform? What trends do we identify in those gaps?
   • Of all the expectations we have for student learning, where do we see the greatest opportunity for student growth?

4. *Prioritize as individuals.* Have each team member read the list and draw a star next to one or two challenges they feel are the most important and urgent to address as a team. Leading this first as a silent activity before discussion supports personal reflection and ensures both extroverts and introverts have an active role in prioritizing the team focus. Encourage team-members to choose priorities based on these two questions:

   • Which will be the greatest priority for student learning?
   • Which illuminates the best opportunity for us to deepen expertise and professional practice?

5. *Prioritize as a team.* When all have placed two stars on one or two challenge areas on the list, look together at the main priorities identified by

the team. There may be one, or several with stars. If many, then discuss the options with the goal of coming to agreement on a POP to drive the teams' collaborative work. This may involve debating choices and/or integrating ideas. To explore integration, ask whether any of these challenges work in tandem together? Are there challenges we want to synthesize into a POP statement to guide our work?

For example, a team within one school identified these challenges:

- Many students, especially ELs, don't participate in partner conversations.
- Students struggle with critical reading.
- Teachers want to know how to help every learner excel with rigorous expectations of CCSS aligned reading comprehension tasks.

They then synthesized these into the POP:

"Our students, especially ELs, are rarely participating in critical reading tasks including collaborative conversations about texts. When they do participate, they are focusing only on literal levels of comprehension."

6. *Write and reflect.* Write the POP as a statement describing the challenge or problem to solve. This often involves between one and four sentences, though be flexible with length to articulate what matters to your team. As you write the POP for the team, reflect on how it meets the top three criteria of an effective POP:

1. How does it align with school/district initiatives (umbrella goal)?

2. How is it an opportunity for student learning?

3. How is it an opportunity for teacher learning?

ASKING QUESTIONS TO DRIVE INQUIRY

"The number one difference between a Nobel Prize winner and others is not IQ or work ethic, but that they ask bigger questions."

—Peter Drucker

Identifying a problem is the first step. What really drives inquiry are the questions. After identifying a POP, generate unanswered questions embedded in that challenge. Ask, "What questions do we hope to answer through our work together?" Write questions about students to help us better understand the challenge or about instruction to help us identify what we might do to make an impact.

Sample Questions About Students (Formative Assessment Questions)

- What can students understand and do in relation to the goal? When students don't do what we expect in a lesson or struggle with a task, what do they do? What do they say? What does this tell us about their thinking? Conceptual understanding? Academic language use? Mindset for learning?
- How do _____ engage in key lesson tasks? (Specify student subgroup that is a priority in your team inquiry, such as black males, ELLs, girls).
- What variations are there in how different students participate, engage, and learn in our classrooms? Are variations random by individual student or are there trends relevant to a subgroup we are trying to address?

Sample Questions About Instruction

- What instructional approaches are most effective in helping students excel with _____?
- How might we personalize instruction during a lesson to meet the needs of all learners?
- How might we foster independent, creative thinking while simultaneously providing scaffolds to students who need support?
- When do scaffolds help students move forward, and when do scaffolds hold them back?
- How do we structure deep discourse among students so students think critically and build up ideas together to deepen expertise with content learning goals?
- How do we support academic language learning in the context of rigorous lessons?

These are examples of questions that drive my continuous learning in education. Every time I find an answer, the new knowledge deepens my curiosity and leads me to more questions. Notice that unanswered questions that matter are not "why" questions about causes beyond a schools' control. They are questions we can pursue through collaborative inquiry together: by testing approaches, watching students, and collaborating to make sense of what the data means.

Examples of Team Questions: Math

Umbrella Goal: Elevate students' critical thinking and problem-solving capacities.

POP: Problem solving is especially challenging for our underperforming students. They often don't seem to understand what is being asked, but instead choose numbers from the problem and try an operation to solve them quickly. When asked to justify their answers, many point at the algorithm they solved. They struggle to analyze and discuss the problem with precision.

Aligned Inquiry Questions

- How do students approach solving problems?
- When they face a challenge, how do they respond? What does what they say and do tell us about their understandings, thinking, and approach to learning?
- How do students justify their responses? Do they use mathematical reasoning? Do they use precise math terms? If they struggle with justifying, are their challenges related to conceptual understandings, reasoning skills, academic language, or a combination of these?
- What types of tasks engage all students in justifying their mathematical thinking in meaningful ways?
- How might we provide the optimal balance of modeling, scaffold, and open-ended problem solving to engage diverse learners in effective independent thinking?

Example of Team Questions: Reading Achievement of Students in Poverty

Umbrella Goal: Elevate literacy achievement for all Academic English Learners, especially students in poverty.

POP: A high percentage of students in poverty are underperforming in reading comprehension relative to their peers. As teachers we want to know more about how students in this subgroup who are struggling in reading complex texts, and how to shift instruction to collectively meet their needs.

Aligned Inquiry Questions

- How do students engage with classroom reading tasks? Do they ask questions, annotate, and/or refer back to the text? In what specific ways are they successful? In what specific ways do they struggle?
- Which strategies are most effective in meeting our students' reading comprehension needs?

- How might we effectively differentiate instruction to engage every learner across a range of levels in our diverse classrooms?

Example of Team Questions: Creativity in Academic Disciplines

Umbrella Goal: Increase opportunities for students to develop creativity across all academic disciplines.

POP: Few students graduate our high school prepared to thrive with the creative demands of 21st-century careers. In core academic content areas, students have limited opportunities to think and act creatively.

Aligned Inquiry Questions

- What is creativity, as it relates to our content instruction?
- How do students engage in creative tasks? Do they think beyond the box of the familiar or focus on creating "the answer" of what they think the teacher expects?
- How might we most effectively engage students in thinking and acting creatively in ways that enhance content learning?

Curiosity Without Bounds

In all of the previous examples, teams generated three or more questions to drive inquiry. This doesn't mean teams need to generate the same number. Sometimes a team narrows their focus on one key question to explore and benefits from a narrow focus. Other times a team writes multiple questions to pursue. Don't limit curiosity to numerical expectation, as quality matters more than quantity. What is most important is that teachers are asking questions to drive learning. Write down the questions that matter most right now, and plan to revisit and revise the list as you continue to learn together. Questions, like creativity, can be unruly. They take us to unexpected places where new questions await.

Write Questions to Drive Inquiry

Purpose: This activity helps teams generate unanswered questions relevant to their POP to focus their OI for the year.

Materials

- This chapter
- Team POP
- Self-stick notes

Directions

1. Explain that the purpose of this activity is to generate questions that inspire professional curiosity and learning specific to our POP. Read Firestein's quote on questions at the beginning of this chapter.

2. Share examples of team questions from the previous section. Engage participants in distinguishing the two question types from the examples: (1) questions about students and (2) questions about instruction. Explain they will generate either or both types of questions.

3. Establish norms of an effective brainstorm especially to accept all ideas, avoid judgment, and share all ideas before discussion.

4. Have all members reread the POP the team has written, and then take time silently to write questions on self-stick notes (one question per note). Encourage questions that either don't have obvious answers, or that have answers in theory or research that we wrestle with making a reality in daily practice.

If helpful, provide starters such as the following:

About Students

- How do students ...?
- What do students say when ...?
- What do students do when ...?

About Instruction

- How *might* we ...?
- How will (instructional action) impact ...?

5. After all participants have time to write one or two questions, have team members share the questions they wrote and put them in a central location for all to see. At this step, share without discussion.

6. Group the brainstormed questions by similarities. If any can be combined, combine them. Cluster questions about students together and questions about instruction together.

7. Prioritize. Have each team member draw a star on up to two questions that they most want to answer through OI. Discuss the options inviting divergent opinions and perspectives. Create together a list of (1–5) questions the team agrees are important to pursue.

(Continued)

(Continued)

8. Publish for team reference. Type the questions on the same document as POP and share with all team members. You will reference this document together at the start of every OI team meeting.

9. Optional: Consider generating one focused question together that incorporates the goal, how success will be measured, and a proposed approach to test (theory of action). A frame that helps drive this type of question is, "How might we (student learning goal), as measured by (task/assessment), by (theory of action)" (Zwiers et al., 2014)? For example, how might we advance students' problem-solving skills, as evidenced by performance tasks by engaging students in collaborative conversations and writing tasks when reading complex texts?

FACILITATION CHALLENGES AND SOLUTIONS

When we facilitate teams in identifying a POP and writing questions for inquiry, our main job is to ask questions to drive the conversation toward what matters *most* to teachers and students. The emphasis on what matters makes this a motivating process that often runs itself. Engaged in exploring their priorities, most teams work collaboratively to find a POP that reflects their top priorities. That said, there could be challenges.

The facilitation challenges that can arise at this stage usually fall into one of two categories: (1) disagreement about what to prioritize or (2) the focus of the POP.

When Team Members Don't Agree on the Priority

Imagine team members brainstorm two or more different ideas, and then don't agree on which should be the POP. It's a common scenario, and often teams come to their solutions through discussion. Other times, they need help engaging in productive debate about the options and coming to agreement about a shared collaborative focus.

When there is a disagreement, help create space for different perspectives to be heard and considered. Disagreement is an asset to team learning, as it challenges each of us to think in new ways. Lydotta Taylor reminds us, "Conflict is a positive force that spurs innovation, helps bring together disparate ideas and diversity of thought" (Armstrong, 2014, p. 3). One way to support productive conflict is to build a culture that values the perspective of every individual, regardless of experience or expertise. My dad, a PhD scientist, always told me "I can always learn something from anyone in the room." His mantra is a good mindset to foster in teams learning together. A veteran teacher can learn from a novice. A principal can learn from a teacher. An education "expert" can learn something from every student and every teacher in every school. We listen, especially when others challenge our thinking. We listen to understand. When "stuck" at a point of disagreement, think of it like a knot in a rope. If we tug at our different perspectives, the knot only gets tighter. When we listen, allowing space for our different perspectives, we move to the center of the knot and open it up.

Evaluate options. We can help facilitate productive discourse about different ideas presented by referring back to the three features of a strong POP and asking questions to help a team evaluate the options.

1. Alignment with school/district

   Ask, "Are our choices aligned to initiatives and priorities we are working on as a site/district?" "Do they align with the umbrella goal?"

2. Opportunity for student learning

   Revisit the data to illuminate priorities. Ask, "In which of these areas do students demonstrate the greatest struggle?" "Which challenge, if we address it together, will have the most significant impact on student learning?"

3. Opportunity for teacher learning

   Evaluate the options based on the question, "Which area do we feel most confident addressing right now with current approaches? Which focus gives us the greatest opportunity to advance our teaching expertise?"

Look beneath the surface. When deciding between two POP focus areas that are equally important for student learning, the teacher learning questions are especially helpful for illuminating the best choice. These questions also surface a dynamic that can be at the root of disagreements: diversity in how team members approach a challenge.

Imagine, for example, a team has narrowed down the options to two strong contenders for a POP focus, both of which are equally justified by student data as priorities for student learning. The first is a POP most teachers on the team feel confident teaching and addressing (e.g., reading fluency). The second is a POP that feels more daunting to teachers (e.g., inferential comprehension).

Debate over which is a bigger priority for a POP may really be a debate over, let's stay in a comfort area together versus let's push the edge of our learning.

This debate, when fueling a surface discussion about which student challenge to address, can have some real teeth as fear is involved. This is the emotion elephant we focused on in Chapter 3, and one we can address productively by creating and maintaining an environment in which teams feel safe pushing the edge of their learning.

When a debate centers on the deeper issue of collaborative risk taking, help surface the issue by shifting the conversation from student learning opportunities to teacher learning opportunities. Ask of the choices under debate, any of the following questions:

- Which of these areas creates the greatest opportunity for our learning as teachers?
- Which of these options do we feel the *least* confident addressing right now in our classrooms? In which would we like to deepen our expertise?

Or explain this:

Your time is precious, and I want to make sure that the time we focus together going deep into one POP area is a powerful learning opportunity for all of us. If we choose a problem that we already know how to solve or questions to which we already have the answers, we risk simply confirming what we already know and wasting our collaborative time. Our goal is to choose a challenge that is a challenge for students and a challenge for us.

Facilitate synthesis. Debating, discussing, and coming to agreement on a choice is one way to resolve a disagreement. Another option is to look for opportunities to synthesize ideas. Look at the top priorities being considered by the team and ask, "Are their unifying features across these ideas? Would it be advantageous to combine any of these challenges into one POP?

For example, consider these two ideas for a team's POP:

- Our ELLs struggle with classroom conversations. Many don't participate or only share an "answer" in highly structured conversation tasks. They don't extend the conversation with peers.
- Students struggle with inferential reading comprehension, especially the CCSS expectations to make and justify inferences with text evidence.

Are there unifying features between these? Are there unifying features across these ideas? Would it be advantageous to combine these into one POP? Try it before reading on.

One example synthesis of these ideas is this: "Many students, especially our ELLs, struggle with reading comprehension tasks in which they are asked to make and justify inferences with text evidence. In classroom conversations about texts, some ELLs don't participate and others respond only to highly structured tasks eliciting an 'answer.'" An aligned question to drive inquiry might be, "How do we structure student conversations about texts in ways that engage every learner in deepening inferential understandings of texts?"

Synthesis in this example is an improvement over either original idea because it helps focus each separate POP into something more specific. We aren't just looking at the broad goal of reading comprehension, but reading comprehension as it relates to collaborative conversations and ELL engagement. We aren't just addressing conversations globally, but conversations in the specific and challenging academic context or reading.

POP Focus Challenges

Another potential challenge teams can have at this stage is they choose a POP that is too broad or narrow to drive productive yearlong work. A facilitator attuned to this issue makes a difference by asking a targeted question to help teams find a focus that is broad enough to address a high-priority challenge in student learning and specific enough to drive lesson planning.

Challenge	Why a Problem?	Solution Strategies
POP is too general.	A very general POP can be a problem when it comes to planning a lesson, as there are way too many possibilities. Example of a general POP: Students struggle with reading.	Ask, what will success with this challenge look like? Get specific. Identify a task students will do to demonstrate success, a task that now is a challenge for many. Use the task to envision the goal and challenge with a new level of specificity. Rewrite the POP to narrow the focus.
Too narrow in focus on one low-level skill.	A narrow focus can be valuable, and also can be problematic if the focus is so narrow it loses the leverage to significantly impact student learning.	Ask, if we address this problem, will it make a significant difference in student achievement?

(Continued)

(Continued)

Challenge	Why a Problem?	Solution Strategies
	A narrow focus is especially problematic when it focuses on a low-level skill out of the context of the high-level application of that skill. For example, "Students often neglect to put a period at the end of their sentence."	When a POP narrows in on a skill, ask questions to broaden the frame of reference from isolation to integration. Ask, in what academic contexts do students most struggle with this skill?
	A POP is also too narrow when it can be learned in one lesson, and there are further opportunities to take the learning deeper.	Revise the POP to include the high-level thinking contexts when students must apply the skill.

REFLECTION QUESTIONS

- What unanswered questions fuel your curiosity for professional learning? What problems of practice do you want to solve?
- How will you engage others in collaborating to identify a POP and questions to drive OI?
- How will you align the inquiry work of teams to site or district initiatives? What steps will you take to ensure OI is not "one more thing" but a *process* for realizing success with what matters most to students, teachers, and schools?

5 Planning for Inquiry

"Plan with the end in mind."

Stephen Covey (2013)

From a problem of practice (POP) and inquiry questions, teams begin to plan their first lesson to observe together. Using a backward planning (Wiggins & McTighe, 2005) approach, we begin with a focus on the end goal and get specific together about these questions:

1. What are our goals for student learning? (Goals)

2. How will students demonstrate success? (Assessment and Success Criteria)

3. What instruction will we provide to ensure student success? (Instruction)

These three questions frame the organization of this chapter, a how-to guide for facilitators to support teams in planning for inquiry.

GOALS FOR STUDENT LEARNING

Begin planning by defining the end goal. Ask, "If we succeed with our POP, what will students know and be able to do?" Then use grade-level content area standards and curriculum to get more specific about the level and context of team expectations.

From a POP, goals begin at a general level. For example, consider this POP identified by a 9th- and 10th-grade math team:

Problem solving is especially challenging for our underperforming students. They often don't seem to understand what is being asked, but instead choose numbers from the problem and try an operation to solve them quickly. When asked to justify their answers, many point at the algorithm they solved. They struggle to analyze and discuss the problem with precision.

At a general level, goals include phrases from the POP restated in the positive:

- Students analyze word problems to identify what is being asked, and solve problems strategically.
- Students justify their reasoning with precision.

General goals from a POP frame the planning, and can also be so broad or include so many elements a team doesn't know where to start for one lesson to plan-observe-teach together. The next step to move toward specificity is to use standards, curriculum, and shared expertise to clarify what success with the goal will look like.

ASSESSMENT AND SUCCESS CRITERIA

Team members collaborate to specifically define the task(s) students will do by the end of instruction to demonstrate success and how they will measure that success. Teams plan this task based on the grade-level and content-area expectations, not where students are currently performing or expected to perform after a lesson or two. The goal is to aim high and be specific about what realizing that level of success will look like.

Key Questions

- If we realize success with our POP, what will success look like?
- What task(s) will students perform to demonstrate success?
- What will we look for to know if they succeeded?
- What types of evidence will be most formative?
- What criteria will we use to measure success?

Think beyond the lines of formal assessments when answering these questions. Depending on your POP and goals, the assessment task(s) a team chooses to measure success will vary widely. Some will be teacher created, and others will be tasks pulled directly from a curriculum or local assessment. A task might involve writing, reading, speaking, listening, collaboration, and/or technology use. There are no limits, only the parameters that the task aligns with the team's goal. What students say and do to complete the task will be evidence of their success (or instructional needs) with the goal.

Sometimes a team creates an assessment task, and other times we can select a task from the curriculum or assessments we are using. Whether we create it from scratch is less important than the alignment between the task and our ultimate goal for student learning.

Getting Specific Together. The primary reason to identify an end assessment task to drive planning is to get specific as a team about our vision for student success. We need specificity about our destination before we can effectively collaborate to get there. Consider, for example, the possible challenge of collaborating to plan a lesson with the goal of inferential reading. What does "inferential reading" mean in terms of what students say and do in a lesson? What task will students do to demonstrate success? Compare your idea to these to possible tasks:

- Students read and annotate a complex informational text then engage in an extended conversation with peers about inferential understandings.
- Students reread a narrative that has been read aloud then answer an inferential reading question asked by the teacher.

Think about this: What do students need to understand and be able to do to excel with each task? How are expectations similar or different? Which task more closely aligns with your vision for what students must be able to do at the grade level(s) you impact to thrive with inferential reading?

Imagine if we sat down to plan a lesson on inferential reading comprehension before getting clear about the end goal. One person imagines the first example. Another imagines the second. While both tasks have to do with the POP, each will lead us to very different approaches in planning and instruction. If we don't collaborate to define the goal together in terms of a specific task, we end up having planning conversations in which each person has a different idea of where we are headed. This leads to disagreements about tasks and strategies, parallel conversations, or surface-level planning. To impact student learning together, we must get specific together about our end goal.

Pre- and Postassessment Tasks. Clarifying a task through which students will demonstrate success focuses planning, and it also helps teams establish a way to measure the impact of their collaborative work. For example, a team focused on the goal of having students summarize key ideas from expository text might choose as their assessment task to have students summarize a three-paragraph excerpt from a text. They create the same task with two different texts and use one in the beginning of the year to gather formative data and one in the end of the year to measure growth.

How a team gathers formative data from the first task depends on the type of task. When the preassessment is a written task, teachers can administer it in their classrooms before their first lesson for observation inquiry (OI). They gather baseline data, analyze the results, and ideally have time with their team to analyze work samples together to identify student strengths and needs to inform planning. When teams in OI also meet regularly as grade-level or department-level teams in a PLC process, there is a natural integration of these activities and teams have more time for ongoing collaboration specific to their POP and goals.

When the evidence of learning for a goal (e.g., collaborative conversation skills) lives in the dynamics of the classroom, creating pre- and post-assessment tasks is more complex. In these cases, teams often approach their first lesson observation as an opportunity to gather formative data toward success with the end goal. This does not mean the lesson will be strictly an assessment, but that the team will intentionally structure at least one task through which they can better understand the question: What can our students do now in relation to the goal?

Creating assessments can be a complex science, or quite simple. It helps to take the pressure off teams by remembering the goal isn't to create a scaled, standardized, publishable assessment from scratch. The goal is to get specific about the end goal and where students are now in relationship to the end goal. Plan the task or task(s) that will help your team see how students perform with your end goal. Plan tasks that give your team insight into what students can and cannot do so you can use that information to drive instructional choices.

Aiming High for Equity. A common planning challenge in contexts where students are currently underperforming is to lower the bar for the end goal. This is a complex issue, especially when teachers come from different socioeconomic, cultural, and linguistic backgrounds than students. Setting low expectations often comes from either fear of making students uncomfortable or fear of making ourselves uncomfortable by focusing on a goal we don't know we can achieve.

Uncertainty especially is a given when there is a large gap between where our students are and where they need to be. It is normal to feel the discomfort of uncertainty when we hold the bar much higher than current levels of achievement. Harness that uncertainty for more questions. Let it drive collective curiosity and learning.

Fear of uncertainty equals fear of failure.

What we cannot afford to do is let an adult fear of failure lower the end goal for students. If our fear leads to a lowering of expectations, we create a tragic situation in which adult fear of failure guarantees students fail.

If you work in an environment where students or a group of students have traditionally underperformed, you know that having high expectations requires more than a belief. It requires 100% commitment and dedication to push the edge of our learning and students' learning every single day. There is no silver bullet. We must be advocates and relentless visionaries moving from challenges toward ambitious solutions.

When a team sets a low bar for the end goal, a facilitator can illuminate the gap in expectations by engaging teams in comparing their end goal to grade-level expectations generated from sources beyond the team. Depending on the context and goal, helpful sources may include

- standards;
- grade-level exemplars from district, state, or CCSS;
- tasks on district or high-stakes tests;
- expectations from the next grade level(s); and
- characteristics expected by employers in the 21st-century economy (Friedman, 2005; Wagner, 2012)

Unpack standards, assessment tasks, or exemplars to illuminate the expectations every student must realize to excel with the specific POP the team has identified together. These activities help a team get tangible and very specific about what success looks like and how they will measure success.

Help reframe statements such as, "Our kids can't do that," by asking, "What instruction and learning opportunities might help them build this capacity?" "What instruction might we provide to ensure student success?" Be prepared to teach the first lesson a team plans, even if you don't have a classroom of your own, to model the risk taking essential for raising the bar and extending possibility. No matter how the lesson turns out, if you begin with high expectations you will either demonstrate that kids can rise to the challenge or create opportunities for teachers to gather specific formative data about what strengths students bring to the task and how they struggle to drive the next level of planning.

PLANNING INSTRUCTION

With clarity about the end goal and assessment task, the team then predicts what instructional approach(es) will help students achieve that goal, and specifically which approach to test together via OI. Another name for this hypothesized solution is a theory of action (TOA) (City, Elmore, Fiarman, & Teitel, 2009). When brainstorming a TOA, consider the following questions:

- What research-based practices address this goal?
- What practices do we know from experience can be successful?
- What approaches have we read about or learned that we want to try?
- What approaches are we attempting but struggling to implement?
- What do we hypothesize will have the greatest impact?

When teams focus on a POP aligned to district initiatives, often they share workshop experiences or readings that they build on to identify a TOA. This is the ideal opportunity for teachers to identify strategies they understand are effective, but are not yet using in practice. Many of the teams in this book, for example, focus on the goal of elevating academic discourse in their classrooms. They already understood the value of engaging students in academic conversations, and yet struggled with the how. Teachers were looking for ways to translate the theory of classroom conversations into effective, practical daily practice.

Ground Planning in Specifics

At a general level, their TOA is to structure peer-to-peer conversations to advance language in tandem with content. In planning a specific lesson, a team narrows in on what, when, and how of what they want to test; for example, one team might focus on think-pair-share or on explicitly teaching students specific discourse skills (Zwiers, O'Hara, & Pritchard, 2014) in extended academic conversations. A team also aligns the goal of conversations to an academic content area or literacy context, such as closely reading complex texts to think critically about author's purpose or solving mathematical problems and articulating justifiable arguments.

In planning the first lesson, it helps to ground the conversation in specifics of context. Clarify, for example, the following:

- Which classroom?
- Which students?
- Which date and time?
- What will students be studying at that time?

- What are the learning progressions between where students are now and our ultimate goal?
- Where will be the most logical place to start this process together?

Schedule Planning Time According to Needs

There are a range of possible approaches to planning and time frames needed. As detailed in Chapter 2, OI typically engages teachers in less up-front planning time than lesson study. This is especially the case when teams are focused on a student learning goal that is centered in the dynamics of instruction such as, advancing academic conversations, building language in tandem with content, ensuring active participation of culturally and linguistically diverse learners in every lesson task, or fostering student initiative and risk taking.

These goals, essential for equity, involve a different mindset for planning than teaching a concrete content objective, such as fractions. When we teach fractions, we plan a unit to build the concept of fractions and a lesson within that unit to address this specific priority-learning goal. However, when we teach academic conversations in the context of mathematical lessons, our planning focus is about layering language, discourse, and interaction on top of a content goal.

Planning the first lesson is the most time-intensive, as a team collaborates to get specific about the goal, what success will look like, and hypothesizes a plan of action for success. All of these essential activities for building background take time. Schedule a minimum of two hours for initial planning and increase the time if a team is gathering materials from multiple sources and designing a lesson from scratch.

When equity is the goal, often teams choose a lesson within an existing curriculum, or pedagogy learned from a workshop, and collaborate to adapt and modify the approach to elevate achievement for diverse learners. In such situations, teams don't design the lesson from scratch, but design/refine an approach to ensure culturally and linguistically diverse learners succeed.

For example, one kindergarten team focused on the goal of engaging all learners, especially ELLs, in discussing nonfiction texts read aloud. They selected a read aloud and determined together the modeling, visuals, and interactive tasks they would use to engage every child in understanding the text at literal and inferential levels. In each subsequent lesson they planned together, they refined their general approach for working with a read aloud while also applying it to the specifics of a different text.

A cross-disciplinary middle school team focused on elevating AEL achievement with open-ended tasks collaborated to enhance content

Possible Planning Challenges and Facilitation Solutions

Challenge: The team begins planning tasks that don't align with the POP. This happens sometimes when teams get excited about a topic or idea and then start planning different possible ways to explore that idea. For example, in a kindergarten and first-grade team focused on the challenge of engaging students in talking about text details, teachers selected *The Mitten* by Jan Brett as a read aloud for the inquiry lesson. As soon as they had selected this text, teachers excitedly shared many different ways to engage students in understanding the story. They generated discussion questions about the story that were all about prior knowledge and personal experience. Not one task for the lesson expected students to discuss text details, the team's POP.

Possible Solution: Validate what you see, and ask a question to prompt new thinking.

I acknowledged the power of engaging students in discussing prior knowledge to deepen comprehension, and asked the team to reread the POP together. After we read it, I referenced the POP and asked a question: "As a team we identified that one of the biggest challenges is engaging students in talking to peers using details from the text. Which tasks in our lesson will help us understand and/or address this challenge?"

One team member reflected aloud that none of the pair-share tasks they had planned involved a discussion of text details. The team then collaborated to change two of the discussion tasks. They also kept a discussion question that focused on prior knowledge, and this is important. Teaching is about synthesis of best practices. We don't throw away an effective strategy for comprehension just because it isn't part of our POP or TOA. We do shift the emphasis, however, so that our lesson modeling and tasks *focus* on our student outcome goal.

Challenge: We run out of time. Despite our best intentions, we sometimes find that the clock turns faster than our facilitation plans. This especially can happen at the lesson planning stage as multiple variables involved impact how long it takes to collaboratively plan a lesson.

Possible Solutions: Use the previous tips to keep planning efficient, and use a timekeeper to stay aware of time. Also determine if there is an option for the team to meet again for planning before the lesson. If the latter is an option, schedule a planning meeting within a week of the actual lesson. Teachers often prefer to plan as close to the lesson date as possible so they can use current data about students to best match scaffolds and modeling to their needs.

If a second planning meeting is not an option, focus on the teacher lead and ask what he or she specifically would like to work out with the team before teaching the lesson. Make those specifics your top priority in the remaining team planning time. Follow up with the teacher to see if he or she wants additional support with final details before the lesson.

Once the team has done at least one lesson together, I often find, even when we are short on planning time, the teacher lead feels like he or she has enough specifics about the next lesson to teach it.

REFLECTION QUESTIONS

- Which aspect of planning do you anticipate will be the biggest challenge for a team? Why? What steps will you take to support their success?
- In your context, how much time do you anticipate teams will need to plan the first lesson?
- How might you schedule time within your context to ensure teams have the collaborative planning time they need to begin OI?

6 Observing Together

"There is no more powerful way of improving on the job than by observing others and having others observe us."

—Roland Barth (Barth, 2006)

O bserving lessons together is at the heart of our process and the most essential step to get right. How we watch student learning, the notes we take, and evidence we share determine the depth of our collaborative learning. To learn in ways that shift our practice, we must hone our skills in observing with an inquiry mindset: to identify evidence that answers our questions and ideally leads us to ask even more.

How we approach observing together determines safety for collective risk taking. The tone we set in observing and debriefing drives the growth mindset that is essential for engaging every team member in teaching in front of colleagues while pushing the edge of new learning.

This chapter is about watching and listening to students, one of the most important skills for effective teaching. It prepares us for the content of the next two chapters: discussing and analyzing what we see to reflect and refine how we teach. The depth of our discussions after an observation hinges on how well we observe and the specific student data we identify to share.

In this chapter, we'll explore observing together in four sections:

1. Focusing the observation

2. Taking descriptive notes

3. Formative evidence examples

4. Using video

FOCUSING THE OBSERVATION: THE PRELESSON MEETING

There are a myriad of details we notice and could write about when watching a lesson. Take any group of educators into a classroom and ask them to take notes on what they see and the details will vary widely. People look for what interests them or seems important based on prior experience observing or being observed. If you are used to using a checklist for observing lessons, for example, your notes will likely emphasize items from that list. If you are concerned about how to manage your students, you will likely notice details related to management. If you are fascinated by ways to integrate critical thinking into lessons, you will especially notice the types of thinking students are doing. We see what we look to see. We notice what we feel is important, or what surprises us.

Note taking during a lesson is easier and most productive for the team when we focus our observation collaboratively on our shared purpose for inquiry. Our goal is to gather student evidence that gives us insight into our problem of practice (POP) and the inquiry questions we hope to answer.

Teams meet briefly before observing together in a 20-minute meeting for two primary purposes: (1) reinforce safety for the teacher teaching the lesson by providing a chance to talk with observers and remember the goal isn't perfection and (2) to read the POP and focus questions to help observers remember the priorities for observation. Use Figure 6.1 for a note-taking template the teacher teaching the lesson (aka teacher lead) uses to prepare for and lead this meeting.

Focus. A team first rereads the POP and unanswered questions together to remember what types of student data to look for. It is helpful to ask, "Given what we want to know, what types of student evidence will be most helpful to gather?" Team members then brainstorm the specific types of evidence they want to gather to understand their problem and answer questions. For example, a team addressing the challenge that ELLs struggle to justify their thinking with text evidence in classroom conversations will prioritize gathering quotes on what ELLs say during justification tasks and also details on if, when, and how students reference back the text in discussions.

Priority students. Typically observers spread out in a classroom to each observe students in different parts of the room. Sometimes, in the prelesson meeting, the teacher lead will assign observers specific students or table groups to watch. Identifying specific students to watch

Figure 6.1 Note-Taking Template

Note-Taking Template: Lead the Prelesson Meeting

Directions: When you are the teacher lead, copy this page and complete it. Use it as a guide in the prelesson meeting.

Teacher Lead: _____ Grade: _____ School:_____

1. **Choose a colleague to reread the team's problem of practice (POP) and questions for inquiry.**
2. **State the learning objective(s) for today's lesson:** *"Students will be able to ..."*

_____

_____

_____

_____

3. **Review together what types of observational data will be most formative for the team to deepen understandings about the POP and inquiry questions** (e.g., student quotes, who participates, how students respond in the moment of challenge, etc.).
4. **Determine which students or table of students each observer will watch.**

＊＊＊＊＊＊＊＊＊＊＊＊＊＊＊＊＊＊＊＊＊＊＊＊＊＊＊＊＊＊＊＊＊＊＊

5. **Optional.** A teacher lead may opt to share a specific professional learning goal relevant to the POP, and ask observers to look for data specific to that goal. Only include the following if valuable to you:

Share a professional learning priority: *"It is my goal to effectively ..."*

_____

_____

Request an observation focus: "I especially want observers to notice/watch for ..."

_____

_____

in advance is especially beneficial when a team is seeking information about a subgroup of students (e.g., ELLs at intermediate proficiency level, students who struggled on a recent assessment, or students identified as gifted and talented). The teacher lead specifically chooses students who are struggling in some way relevant to the POP. The goal is not to focus on students most likely to succeed in a lesson, but instead to watch students whose actions and thinking will give observers the most insight into the POP.

Norms. In the prelesson meeting, briefly review norms the team developed for effective observations. The following are examples of team norms:

- Write descriptions, not judgments.
- Be a fly on the wall. Don't interact with students even if they appear to need help.
- Sit close enough to hear students talking to one another, but not so close that you distract. If students appear distracted by your presence, move back or to another part of the room.
- Don't discuss the lesson until our team debrief. No hallway talk.

A mindset for growth. Even after building initial trust and getting comfortable taking turns teaching while others observe, it helps to remain cognizant of the fear that is a natural response to feeling "on the spot" when anyone teaches in front of colleagues. Since observing always means another teacher is stepping into the risk-taking role of teacher lead, approach observation with the elephant in mind.

One way we lower anxiety is by keeping the focus on the students, and also by reminding one another to only gather and share descriptive evidence. In the prelesson meeting, a facilitator also helps ease pressure by reminding the team that teaching the perfect lesson is never the goal.

Before a lesson I often remind a team, "When we are the ones teaching we always want the lesson to be seamless, but really when a lesson has bumps and unexpected moments of student struggle, it is a gift to our team process. These moments are when we get the best insights into student thinking and learning."

The teacher about to teach usually laughs at this and says, "Don't worry, there will be bumps. It won't be perfect!"

This sets the right tone for a growth-focused observation. We walk to the classroom together: a team focused on a shared understanding that we are watching students in a moment of learning and welcoming the imperfections that are part of pushing the edge of what we know.

TAKING NOTES IN A LESSON

Our task as observers is to sit by one or more students during the lesson and take notes on what they say and do. After observing, we'll review our notes and prioritize five specific details from our notes to share with our team.

Since we share select data from our notes, not the notes themselves, the format of the actual notes doesn't matter. Each team member may have a preferred approach to taking notes (e.g., paper, laptop, with or without columns), and all formatting approaches are valid. What matters is the content. In taking notes we always prioritize writing specific, descriptive details about students that will help us understand and address our POP.

It's About the Students

The most important information observers gather focuses on the students: what they say and do in a moment of learning. To deepen understandings with our POP and the impact of our instructional moves, we need student data. We watch and note student actions and speech to answer key questions relevant to our team. At a general level, these questions often include the following:

- What do students say?
- What do students do?
- Who participates?
- How do students approach a task?
- How do students interact?
- How do students respond to a specific scaffold or instructional move?

Notice these questions all focus on students, not the teacher. We are not asking, "Does the teacher use this or that strategy?" or "Is the objective on the board?" We seek specific student evidence to help us understand when and how students learn (or don't learn). Even the last question, which calls for a focus on teaching, emphasizes the impact on students.

This is a mindset shift for some observers, and an important one to make. Our emphasis shifts from delivery to learning. There is no benefit from studying teaching (a means) in isolation from learning (the end). We want to study and discuss how our teaching impacts student learning. To do so, we must get specific about students.

Teaching and Learning Connections

A focus on students does not mean a complete avoidance of writing details of instruction. While we don't want to take notes on teacher actions in isolation (e.g., the teacher modeled), it is valuable to specify the instructional context of student actions. Consider the following examples:

> With 20 seconds for pair-share, the second student to talk said three words before the time was called.

> After seeing the teacher model the first step on the overhead, every student at the table started completing the organizer.

Instructional context is data that can help a team infer the cause-and-effect link between teacher action and student outcomes. Notice that these examples don't state the inference or make a recommendation. This is important, as the cause-and-effect link is an interpretation, and not allowed in the first step of our debrief protocol. Inference has a role later in the collective process, after the team agrees on the facts. At this first stage of observing, our task is to take notes and prepare to share in the language of evidence. We will make inferences as we observe, as our brains are quick with this process, but we don't write an individual inference such as, "Modeling helped every student start the organizer." The verb helped indicates a judgment. Stating the facts in sequence is a nonevaluative way to describe the same facts. Specificity about students and the instructional context for their actions equips a team with evidence to discuss what happened, what it means, and what can be learned to inform teaching.

Describe Without Judgment

Describing without judgment helps colleagues get specific together about students, and it fosters a climate of team safety and trust. For this reason, it is an essential skill to learn and practice before watching lessons together.

Describing what we see without interpretation or inference isn't an automatic skill for most of us, and it takes intentional practice to master. The good news is that practicing it is fun and beneficial early in the launch workshop to address fears.

Workshop Activity: Distinguishing Description From Judgment (7 minutes)

To establish the safety of nonevaluation, teach and practice the distinction between description and judgment.
Time: 5–7 minutes

Materials:

- Green note cards, on which each participant writes, "What's the evidence?" (City, Elmore, Fiarman, & Teitel, 2009).

Procedure:

1. Briefly explain the difference between a description and a judgment using examples.

2. Choose an object in the room (e.g., bookshelf), and have participants each write a descriptive statement, and a judgment about that object. To encourage subtle distinctions, explain that we will soon play a game to try to guess which is which.

3. Invite teachers to read one statement to the group without specifying whether it is a judgment or a description. Ask listeners to distinguish which it is. When a judgment is shared, have listeners signal with the green note card and ask, "What's the evidence?"

Move from this general activity to practice taking and sharing specific descriptive notes about a video lesson. In this next activity, teachers practice two key observation essentials: describe without judgment and focus on the students.

Workshop Activity: Practice Describing With a Short Video (7 minutes)

Teachers take notes during a one- to two-minute video to practice describing without judgment and focusing on the students.
Time: 8–10 minutes
Materials

- Green note cards, on which each participant has written, "What's the evidence?" (City, Elmore, Fiarman, & Teitel, 2009)
- Paper or laptops/tablets for taking notes
- A short one- to three-minute video of classroom instruction. Choose or create a video relevant to your teaching context and age group in which the camera focuses on students. www.theteachingchannel.org is a great source for videos, and you can also create your own. For this activity, use a section of a lesson that shows students talking, writing, or responding rather than simply listening to a teacher.

(Continued)

(Continued)

Procedure

1. Explain that now we'll practice taking notes in a lesson to practice describing student evidence without judgment. Unlike in the previous activity, now we are only writing descriptions and trying to avoid writing interpretations on the page.

2. Introduce note taking in a way that honors the skills and prior knowledge of the group. A brief introduction is usually best to introduce ideas for formatting and note-taking shortcuts (e.g., T = teacher, S = students).

3. Confirm all are ready to get started. Remind observers to be specific in describing what students are saying and doing. Show the video clip.

4. After the video, have observers read back over their notes and identify one specific piece of descriptive evidence to share.

5. Have partners share evidence to practice both describing and listening for judgments. Remind people that if they hear a judgment to flash the green card and ask, "What's the evidence" or "What did you see that lead you to think that?"

6. Conclude with a short whole-group discussion to share examples of descriptive evidence from the video, and discuss any pieces of evidence that are in the gray area between description and judgment.

With practice, teachers quickly become attuned to listening for judgments. Many internalize the norm and make it a game to notice judgments whenever they arise, even in casual conversations outside the team inquiry process. This shared awareness builds safety. When teams together learn to describe without judgment and hold one another accountable for doing the same, they experience deeper feelings of collaborative trust and increased comfort opening classroom doors.

Navigating the Gray Areas

The description/judgment distinction isn't always cut and dried. Many phrases we use in education to "describe" what we see are general statements dependent on interpretation. For example, consider the following. Are these descriptions or judgments?

- The students are engaged.
- Students are off task.
- Students are using academic language.

When it is difficult to distinguish a description from a judgment, ask, "Is the statement open to interpretation? Might we disagree that it is true?" If yes, it's a judgment.

In a general way, these statements "describe" what's happening in the classroom, but they describe through a lens of interpretation. Let's take the first, for example, engagement. Consider the following scenarios. For each, ask yourself, "Are students engaged?"

- Scenario 1: Students are flicking their pencils and playing with erasers as a teacher explains the task. During the peer-conversation, they have an extended discussion about the lesson content.
- Scenario 2: All students sit-up straight and listen to the teacher. When the teacher asks a question, five raise their hands to speak. One gives the correct answer.

Are the students engaged? Answers to this question are debatable because we may have different criteria for engagement. Defining whether students are engaged is less important than discussing together what they specifically do. It is formative data to know that the students who are flicking pencils participate in the extended conversation about the lesson content. It is formative data to know that when a question is asked, five raise their hands and one student shares a response. This specific information teaches us about the students, their participation, and understanding in response to our instructional moves. The general, evaluative statement "students are engaged" does not.

In an interview with *Education Week,* expert educator Charlotte Danielson revealed the challenge of looking for a general indicator such as engagement in observations. She pointed out that principals often don't recognize real student engagement, "If the students are compliant and doing what the teacher says, if they're on task and busy, principals will often call it 'engaged.' But the students might not be doing any thinking at all. They might just be filling in some blanks on a worksheet" (Rebora, 2013a).

When the only data discussed live in general statements such as, "students are engaged," every person on the team will likely have a different image of what that means. Getting specific is essential for going deeper together. Share evidence of student thinking, interactions, initiative, or actions that illustrate the type of engagement you seek (or are trying to improve). Danielson's example of "students are filling in blanks on a worksheet" is specific classroom evidence that can drive a deeper discussion. Without such data, a conversation about "engagement" does not change anyone's perception or thinking. We only hear and say what we already know.

Be Specific

An easy way to ensure our notes in a lesson describe rather than judge is to be specific.

The more specific we can be, the more formative our data are for the team. Compare the statements in the following table:

General and Debatable	Specific
Kids are off task.	When asked to write, students are talking to each other.
	Three of four students stared at their paper for the first four minutes of the task.
Students are using academic language.	One student said, "Electromagnetic waves transfer energy. It gives off heat and allows us to see."
	Six out of seven students who reported used language to show a cause-and-effect relationship between ideas (e.g., when, because, caused).
	Each student who shared, used the sentence frame, "Based on, _____."

When discussing student's language use, it is especially important to be specific. "Academic language" is too broad of a term. For one person, it may simply mean use of vocabulary or a teacher-provided frame. For another, it involves application of complex sentence construction while explaining a complex idea. As with engagement, we aren't as interested in debating the definition of the general term "academic language" as we are in getting very specific about the language students use.

Seek Evidence of Challenge, Not Just Success

Sometimes people interpret the goal of "describing without judgment" to mean that observers should only take notes on how students are succeeding and leave evidence of struggle out of observation notes. This is not the goal. Evidence that students struggle in a lesson and the details about how they struggle are essential formative data to help us understand students and refine instruction. Ensure team members know that "describe without judgment" does not limit *what* evidence to share, but is only about *how* we share it. We must observe, note, and share any evidence, whether evidence of struggle or success, without such labels. While we don't say, "students struggled," or "students succeeded," we describe precisely the evidence of struggles and success. Evidence of challenges in student learning is our greatest asset for driving team learning. Foster a growth mindset by valuing especially the observation data that reveal an opportunity to deepen expertise.

FORMATIVE EVIDENCE EXAMPLES

The details we take notes on in an observation depend on the POP and questions our team seeks to answer. That said, there are categories of evidence that are formative in any situation, regardless of the learning goal. These include quotes, timing, participation, and process.

Quotes

Student quotes are valuable evidence in any lesson. What students say gives us insight into students' understandings, misunderstandings, curiosity, and attitudes about learning. Quotes are valuable evidence for students' oral language use, discourse skills, and language choices across diverse tasks.

Consider, for example, these excerpts of student quotes shared from lessons in which students are asked to engage in partner discussions to justify a claim. What do these quotes tell you about students? Why might these data be important to a teacher in a lesson or to a team?

1. In the last task of a seventh-grade science lesson, students are asked to defend the statement, "Electromagnetic waves transfer energy." One student reads what she has written to her partner, "One example of when light transfers is when light shines on water it can sometimes make it warm and when you are in the sun too long you get a sunburn." Her partner then reads what he wrote.

2. In a second-grade task to infer and justify how a character feels in a text, two ELL students have the following dialogue. One student says, "Sad. He made his own goal and his team made a face to him." His partner replies, "I disagree because when his face turned red I think it's disappointed."

Reflection on what these quotes reveal about students:

- Understanding of the content or text
- Current capacities to make and/or justify a claim

- Use of language
- Discourse skills

One quote in isolation is a small slice of information. The value of these data multiplies when a team focuses together on gathering quotes relevant to a very specific inquiry question. A team focused on how students infer and justify in partner discussions, for example, will gather quotes during each task requiring inference and justification. What students say helps the team understand how students think about texts, what kind of inferences they make or don't make, and how they justify their ideas. Quotes illuminate the language students use when justifying as well. Do they state each idea in isolation or connect claim and justification with "because" or more complex syntax and connective words?

A different team focused on building students' discussing skills will gather evidence on how students respond to one another's ideas. Do they build up ideas together or just each state a new idea in succession? When they do listen and respond, what discourse moves do they use? Are students asking one another questions or prompting to elicit more information? When there is a disagreement, do partners talk through it or stop? Do they show evidence of learning from what one another says?

Reflection question: What do you listen for when listening to what students say in a classroom? How does what they say inform your understanding of their needs?

Timing

When a lesson involves collaborative student tasks or independent tasks, it is often helpful to notice how students use their time. How students use their time in a task gives us insight into their thinking, their process, and the types of support they may need to thrive with lesson tasks.

Most of all, focusing on timing helps us get specific in describing what we see.

Compare these two descriptions from a partner activity in which the goal was to have students identify and articulate the most important details from a content text. The task the teacher was testing for the first time was to have students collaborate to make a poster of key ideas. Two different ways observers describe the event are as follows:

A. In the partner task, students discuss which marker color to use then which details to write about the text. They write a few words before time is called.

B. Given six minutes for the partner task, the pair spends five minutes discussing which color markers to use, then one minute writing details about the text. They write a few words before time is called.

For each description, reflect on these questions:

- How are these descriptions similar?
- How are they different?
- Which is more formative? Why?

Compare now these two ways of describing events in a fourth-grade lesson on identifying main ideas in a science text. The team was collaborating to address student challenges in summarizing informational text. In this moment of the lesson, every student had read the text, and was taking notes using an iPad.

A. Students each open a note-taking application, choose a format, and type notes about the text. In 14 minutes, half complete the task.

B. After reading, students open a note-taking application, spend 12 minutes adjusting font size and color, and two minutes typing a note about the text. In 14 minutes, half complete the task.

For each description, reflect on these questions::

- How are these similar?
- How are they different?
- Which is more formative? Why?

Participation

In teaching for equity, our goal is to reach every student. In any lesson, it is thus valuable to gather information relevant to participation. For example, when noting what students are doing, also note how many. We can do this whether we focus on the entire class or just a table of students, as is typical in team observations. If you are watching a table of four students, for example, and notice that students refer to the text in their conversation, indicate if 4/4 are doing this or 2/4 are doing this. If the class is chorally reading and you notice that several students are not participating, scan the room to see how many are and how many are not. Each time you describe a student action be as precise as possible about how many students you are watching and how many in that group perform the same action.

Participation data are also qualitative. To effectively reach all learners in diverse classrooms, we don't just want to know how many participate, but who participates and how. When only some students are participating or responding in a certain way, notice who responds in the same way and who doesn't. Ask whether there is a correlation between who participates this way and a subgroup, such as gender, ethnicity, language status, or students qualifying for free or reduced lunch. If there is, identify it as my principal did so clearly in my first year of teaching. After an observation, she pointed out that 5/25 students participated in the whole group discussion. She then got more specific by aligning the numbers to a subgroup trend: All five who participated were boys.

Because she told me more than numbers, I had a powerful "aha" moment about gender inequity I hadn't noticed in my classroom. Had she focused only on numbers, I might not have noticed I was only calling on boys.

As observers, we don't always notice such a trend in the moment, especially when our task is to watch two to four students during the lesson. This is okay. What is important is that when we notice variations in how students participate and respond, we ask questions to better understand those variations. Are the variations in how students respond random, or is there a trend that can help us better understand and meet the needs of all learners?

Notice race. Notice gender. Notice language status. When elevating achievement of students in poverty is a focus, use school data to know which students qualify for free or reduced lunch. Is there an alignment between a subgroup and the participation numbers you see? If yes, name it. If not, stick to the numbers and the specifics of what individual students say and do.

Even when we don't see a trend in our individual observations, the specific data we gather help our team collectively identify trends and generalizations. During a discussion of a lesson, one fifth/sixth-grade team at a charter school noticed that there was variation in how students were using conversation scaffolds during a collaboration task. Three teachers, who each watched different student groups, each reported different findings:

1. Students read from sentence frames every time they spoke. Their conversation mimicked the exact pattern of the teacher model.

2. Students sometimes referenced the sentence frames, and sometimes extended the conversation in their own ways.

3. Students applied the concepts the teacher modeled using their language and conversational moves each time.

The team first interpreted these data at a general level: There is a range in how students use the scaffolds in their conversations.

Then they asked specifically who was in each different group and noticed a trend. There was a direct correlation between English language proficiency (as tested by the CELDT test, a measure of English proficiency used in California schools) and use of scaffolds during this lesson task. The students who mimicked the teacher were students with emerging proficiency in English. The second had tested at the intermediate or expanding level of English. The third group that engaged beyond the scaffolds had advanced or bridging levels of English proficiency.

Gathering data at this level of specificity shifted the team conversation from "some kids rely on scaffolds, what can we do about it?" to "how do we effectively differentiate to meet the needs of students at each EL proficiency level? How do we build a strong progression from initially using scaffolds to thriving with independent application?"

Practice: Watch a lesson (or students during your lesson) with an emphasis on participation. Use fractions to take notes of how many students you see participate in that way (e.g., 4/4, 18/25). Also focus on who participates and how. Are there trends?

Process

Other valuable forms of evidence to gather are clues that reveal how students process a learning task. When we watch students attempt a new task, we often gain insights about their thinking and approach—especially when their actions are not what we expect.

If a student doesn't do something "correctly," for example, don't just note that it's incorrect; describe what the student does. If students are talking, write what they say. If they are writing, write what they write. If they are solving a problem or completing a multistep task, describe their approach: What do they do first? Then what? How do they interact with others or with texts as they complete the task?

A Petaluma team of fourth-grade teachers focused on helping English learners excel with inferential reading comprehension gained a valuable insight about process. In their first lesson, the central task was to infer and justify using a graphic organizer to write three key elements: (1) text evidence, (2) prior knowledge, and (3) their inference.

Observing students during the lesson, many noticed that students wrote the inference in the wrong part of the organizer. This observation alone would lead the team toward discussing ways to help students use the organizer correctly.

One team member noticed something else: process. Whether they used the organizer correctly or not, every student she observed wrote the inference first. It was the first step of their process. Some wrote it "correctly," where we asked for it, in the third box of the organizer. Many wrote it in the first box that asked for text evidence. No matter where they wrote it, students wrote the inference first.

This descriptive evidence about student process fueled a different discussion entirely. The challenge wasn't simply that students didn't use the organizer correctly; it was that the organizer didn't match the students' thinking process. The original organizer was based on the assumption that inferring was the hardest skill and students would need a visual scaffold to build from text evidence and prior knowledge to formulate an inference. What the team noticed in the evidence about student process, however, challenged this assumption. Students were making inferences almost instantaneously, especially when working with familiar contexts. Their challenge in the complete task came at the next step: justifying their thinking articulately using text evidence.

With new insights about student process, teachers shifted their approach. Had they only noticed that students failed to use the organizer correctly, they might have only changed how to help students follow directions. Instead, they collaborated to revise the task in ways that specifically aligned with students' current abilities and instructional needs. This collaborative shift is a move toward one of Pedro Noguera's top recommended practices for equity: "teaching the way students learn rather than expecting them to learn by the way you teach" (Rebora, 2013b, para 16).

Notice that all of these details are about students. We don't need details about what is posted on the wall unless we see students referencing it and using it. We don't need lists about what strategies teachers use unless we are describing how students respond to the strategy. For example, it doesn't help the team to have an observer note simply "teacher used pair-share." It is more informative to describe what students say during the pair-share as evidence of understanding, language use, or other elements of learning the team is trying to understand.

In the early stages of building capacity in teams, there are always at least a few people who describe teacher actions in isolation rather than identifying impact on students. A gentle reminder to focus on the students can be helpful, and experience is the most powerful teacher. The first time you go through the process of categorizing notes to make generalizations as a team, participants often have "aha" insights about which data are most helpful to answer the team's questions and address the POP. Observers who have focused only on teacher strategies see first hand that the notes others have written students are the most informative. This is why it is key to practice the protocol more than once and to engage in multiple inquiry cycles around live lessons together. We all sharpen our observations with practice, especially after we experience the formative value of precise observational data.

A Change in Variables

Sometimes we have a golden opportunity as observers to see a distinct shift in how students interact, respond, or participate. In these times especially, it is valuable to get specific about the students *and* the instructional context for their actions. The following are two examples of such evidence.

In the conversation task on a personal topic, four out of four students discussed with elaboration and evidence. In the task about the academic text, three students shared one idea. One was silent.

The students who had been staring at their papers for five minutes started writing immediately after the teacher provided a second example.

For each example, reflect on these questions:

- What is the shift in how students participate?
- What is the shift in instruction or task?
- Why is instructional context an important part of this data?

Noticing how student actions change in two contexts helps educators both understand students and also the cause-and-effect link between instructional choices and student outcomes. In the first example, we learn that a shift from a personal to an academic task leads the same students to different levels of conversation. In analyzing this contrast, we learn more about the skills students have with extended discourse and that they struggle with applying those skills in an academic context involving challenging text. This is the important formative data teachers need to plan lessons that build on students' strengths and address specific needs.

The second example reveals the impact of modeling in this one situation. Students who had been staring at their papers started writing immediately after the teacher came to their table and provided a second example. If we only looked at one piece of this data in isolation, we would only see students not writing (and infer they were lost) or students writing (and infer they understood). By describing the shift in the context of the instruction, we provide our team with data that support cause-and-effect analysis of the impact of teaching on learning.

Planning a Direct Comparison

Observers are not always so lucky to see a change in variables in one lesson, and they have the best shot when planning a comparison of two scenarios intentionally into the lesson. This is a good approach for a team to use when testing the impact of a strategy. A team focused on structuring effective partner conversations, for example, might wish to test the impact of scaffolds on student participation. They could plan the lesson to include one structured pair-share task with modeling and response frames and one without any scaffolds to compare how students interact in each situation. Look in each task to see who participates, what they say, how they interact, and what language choices they make. Compare across the two tasks to see if there is a difference in how students participate, interact, or speak in the structured task compared to the task without scaffolds.

Many teams glean "aha" moments from such observations. In a primary classroom where students were new to partner interactions, the team noticed that participation increased significantly with structured tasks. This insight led teachers on the team to use more structured tasks initially to build student confidence and accountability in partner conversations.

A fifth- and sixth-grade team also compared structured to unstructured tasks and discovered a different result, in part because they asked a different question. Their students could participate in pair-share, but their conversations were predictably following the response frames and structures of the teacher's model. The teachers asked, "How do we engage students in dynamic, student-directed conversations in which they apply skills in their own diverse ways, rather than relying on scaffolds?" When they compared student conversations in structured and unstructured tasks, they noted that without response frames and modeling, many of their students extended their conversations and language use in new ways. Seeing students take risks beyond the scaffolds was a powerful "aha."

Even when we don't plan a direct comparison of strategies in a lesson, there are often opportunities to note shifts in how students respond to the variations that happen in the natural progression of teaching, such as shifts in the level of scaffolding, release of responsibility to students, or reteaching to meet a need. When you do notice a change in what students say or do, be as specific as possible about the instructional variables in each context. What changes from one task to the next? Consider variables including modeling, scaffolds, task complexity, timing, or the use of a specific strategy in one context but not the next. If you see a clear shift in an instructional variable, it may have something to do with the shift in student outcomes; note it.

As the first step of the debrief protocol is to describe, prepare to share evidence that could be relevant to cause and effect without stating a cause-and-effect connection. Rather than using words like "caused," "lead to," or "because," state the facts in sequence or with the frame "When _____, _____." This focus on just the facts helps a team build shared understanding of the facts before making inferences together later in debrief discussion.

USING VIDEO

Video footage of lessons is a convenient professional learning tool for practicing observing and debriefing lessons together and yet has limitations.

Benefits and Limitations of Using Video

Advantage of Video	Disadvantages of Video
• Convenient to share in a presentation or online • Can be used any time of day • Time efficient for short observations within a workshop	• Can sometimes be hard to hear students in peer discussions • One viewpoint for all observers is limited to the focus of the camera • Time-intensive to film and edit, especially when using two cameras to capture teach and students in real time • A video that captures the whole class is rarely close enough to students to show evidence of their learning and understanding

Capturing Formative Videos

When you are creating your video, follow these tips to enhance how video can support professional learning:

- Ensure parents have signed video release forms in advance of filming. Reseat students who don't have permission to participate, or make arrangements for them to be in another classroom during the filming.
- Make sure the camera is not a distraction to students during the lesson. Practice filming before the lesson you film so it becomes routine.
- Focus on students, not just the teacher. Ideally film with two cameras, one focused on the whole class and one focused on students in conversations. Edit the footage together in a cohesive flow (a time-intensive process).
- If filming with one camera, focus on a group of students.
- Use microphones for the students, not just the teacher. One way to do this is to place a remote microphone in the center of a pair or group of students. Another approach is to use a boom microphone on a camera that focuses on students.
- Add subtitles for student conversation, if sound quality is poor.

Why Not Use Video Instead of Live Observations?

With widespread video technology in smart phones, tablets, and afford-able cameras, it is reasonable to also ask if we should just film and watch lessons as a team instead of being in classrooms together. What if we just planned a lesson, had one teacher teach and film it, and then watched it together? While video saves on the logistics of releasing all observers for a live observation, it can limit the data gathered and inhibit risk taking.

Video limits the data observers can gather because a videographer (or tripod) determines the frame of reference for observers. The focus may be limited to a few students or show the whole class in a way that makes it challenging for observers to gather specific and varied formative data from the class. Filming with multiple cameras begins to address this chal-lenge, but requires editing or double the time to watch—two unappealing options for busy educators.

Video as the only method for observing together in continuous plan-teach-reflect cycles can also hinder risk taking. In each lesson, it is important teachers continue to push the edge of their practice. This is the opposite of what most of us want to do when being filmed. There is permanence about video, and others beyond the team may see the footage. Agreements and norms about how footage is used or destroyed after a team meeting could change this, and yet there still can be an extra layer of anxiety among some teachers to teach on film. Many who would take a risk in a safe environment with trusted team members will pause before doing the same thing on video. We wonder who will watch this. What will they be looking for? What will they say when I'm not I the room?

Even if we don't care who else sees the video, there is that other issue: We will watch ourselves. Watching videos of our own practice is a very effective self-reflection and coaching tool. It also takes courage and even more courage if the first time we see the video is with a team who helped plan the lesson. We could address this by watching it before the team, but this just adds to the layers of anticipation and possible anxiety, first to teach on film, then to watch it, then to watch it with colleagues. If we teach a live lesson, we do it once and reflect immediately afterward with our team.

Video in Addition to Live Observations

While using video as the only way to observe together is problematic, using video in tandem with live observations can enhance the process. Teams sometimes choose to integrate video using one of the following approaches:

1. Video for self-reflection: If the teacher who is teaching the lesson wants to film the lesson, we set up a tripod to film it at the same time

colleagues are in the room. The teacher then has the video to watch and can decide whether to delete it or share it.

2. Video to supplement student observations: During the lesson, as observers focus on students, a video camera on a tripod films one group of students. The team watches the video together if more student evidence is needed during the debrief.

The key elements of these approaches are teacher choice, ownership, and decision making about how the footage is used.

Learning by Doing

How we observe and the specific notes we take and share about student learning determine the depth of our collaborative work. Learning what to look for and practicing gathering formative data are important foundational tasks for observation inquiry (OI). Using the videos with the professional learning tools in this chapter, we begin the process. The deep learning begins when we step into classrooms together to apply and refine our observation skills in the context of inquiry. In the next two chapters, we'll explore the protocols for these important next steps.

REFLECTION QUESTIONS

- What do you typically focus on when watching a lesson? What do colleagues in your context typically focus on when observing lessons?
- How will you build the collective capacity of team(s) to focus on evidence that will deepen their understanding of students and the impact of instructional choices?
- How will you ensure safety in how colleagues observe one another?
- Will you use video as a tool for observing lessons together? Why? Why not?

7 Describing and Analyzing What We Observed

"Be intrigued by mistakes, enjoy effort, and keep on learning."

—Carol Dweck (2008)

I magine you planned a lesson with four colleagues and now, you are teaching it as they watch your students and take notes. The lesson isn't going as you had expected. Some students are struggling, and a few are playing with their pencils and laughing about something else. The "aha" moments you'd hoped for aren't happening. When the lesson ends, you and your team walk to a conference room to discuss the lesson.

In this moment, imagine the following:

- How are you feeling?
- What are you thinking?
- What is the first thing you will want to say to your team?
- What protocols will make the lesson discussion both safe for you and powerful for team learning?

Sitting down together to discuss a lesson is a pivotal moment in a team's collaboration. The norms we follow and protocols we use to discuss our observations make or break team trust and learning. Consider the emotional and social dynamics involved in talking about a lesson one of us has taught. For example, after I teach a lesson in front of others, it's my natural impulse to immediately tell observers what didn't go well and what I would have changed. If I follow this impulse and my teammates also follow the social norm to help me feel better by complimenting my teaching, our discussion will deteriorate quickly into a judgment fest. An example of the conversation we don't want to have is here:

Me: "That didn't go well. I wish I hadn't . . ."

Observer 1: "No, it was great. You did a great job!"

Observer 2: "Some kids are always going to have a hard time. They got distracted and you handled it well."

Even a polite exchange of positive compliments is counterproductive as it takes the focus away from student learning and reinforces the idea that observers are in the room to judge the teacher. Compliments are judgments. We love them, but they set up a feedback dynamic that gets in the way of collaborative problem solving and inquiry.

So how do we facilitate a different conversation that builds collective trust while also probing deep inquiry into student data that will push the edge of all of our learning?

Shaping the Conversation

A protocol is a structure we use to guide our approach. It shapes the focus of team observations, and it specifies the steps we follow to share and discuss what we see. It's a support structure for the facilitator and for participants, as it keeps the process focused on the students, the data, and how to move forward together.

Without a protocol, too much is left to chance. Without guidance, there are usually three directions a conversation about a lesson will go:

1. Powerful: Yes, the best outcomes can happen naturally.

2. Superficial: We maintain a culture of nice and skim over opportunities to discuss challenges that can help us grow.

3. Personalized: We share options, often having parallel conversations in which we do more explaining than understanding. Disagreements either lead to debate or silent breakdowns of trust.

In my first year leading teams in observation inquiry (OI), I facilitated with a fluid process rather than a strict protocol. It worked, as long as I was on my toes constantly and using all my facilitation tools: prompting, asking questions, guiding, and redirecting. It worked because of the tone I set and the norms we established, yet it was not scalable. When I tried to release responsibility and have other team members facilitate, I learned how intensively I had been guiding the process. I had made it *my* responsibility to shape the conversation toward powerful, rather than creating a protocol to help the *team* lead itself. Without a protocol, a facilitator shoulders all the challenge of keeping the discussion focused on formative student data and away from, "I like . . ." or "You should have done . . ." feedback. Powerful conversations are possible, but they are entirely dependent on the facilitator or the dynamics of the team. When I used to lead debrief discussions with this less-structured approach, I sometimes felt like a juggler who needed more hands to keep all the balls in the air. In retrospect, it is obvious that this is why I first struggled with the transition of releasing responsibility to other teachers to facilitate.

The following year, we moved to a more structured protocol. The most significant shift was how we approached the first 10 minutes of the debrief conversation: the most crucial minutes to get right. To understand our shift, compare these two scenarios:

A. After the lesson, the teacher lead talks about what worked and didn't work. Team members chime in with observations and ideas.

B. After the lesson, the observers quietly read back over their notes to identify five specific pieces of evidence relevant to the problem of practice (POP). They share descriptions of student actions or speech without adding interpretation or judgment.

Reflect

- How are these similar? How are they different?
- Which feels more natural? Which fosters team safety and trust?
- Which builds a foundation for a deep discussion about student learning?

I began with Scenario A, a standard debrief step in many peer observation processes including peer coaching and Japanese lesson study. In my experience, I find it most natural to let the teacher who taught the lesson begin the conversation. It's a nice release for the teacher to reflect on the experience immediately after teaching. It is also empowering, especially in peer coaching, for the teacher who was observed to be in the driver seat at the start of the conversation.

Yet OI is not about coaching or giving feedback to a teacher. It is about engaging *as a team* in deep inquiry. We are observing lessons to gather data that helps us understand student learning and the impact of instructional

- When you share, remember to only read the description and not to add on an interpretation. This might feel strange as we naturally want to introduce ideas with phrases such as, "This is interesting," or "This was effective." Resist the temptation. Stick to the facts.
- If you hear a judgment or interpretation, ask, "What's the evidence." Or, "What did you see students do that lead you to think that?"

Possible Challenges and Solutions for Facilitators

If . . .	Then . . .
Someone shares a judgment (positive or negative)	Ask, what is the evidence? What did you see students do that led you to that interpretation?
Someone shares a detail relating only to teacher actions (e.g., The teacher modeled)	Ask, what did you see students doing at that time? What did you see students do or say as a result of that instructional move?
The data people share are very general, not specific enough to drive the team inquiry	<ul><li>Ask for more specifics when possible.</li><li>Model specific student evidence in the evidence you share as a guide for the next observation.</li><li>Use recommendations in Chapter 6 to train the team in the types of evidence to gather.</li></ul>
The teacher lead tries to explain a piece of evidence someone else shared, or engage in conversation about it	Acknowledge the interest in discussing details, and assure the team there will be time to discuss specifics later in the protocol. Remind the team the goal now is to come to agreement about what we saw as a foundation for that deeper discussion.
People take turns sharing one note at a time, each share all notes in sequence, or speak out at random times	Be open to however the team naturally shares the notes. As long as each person gets to share and hear all notes before the conversation moves to the next step, it doesn't matter the approach.

It is also possible at this stage for a teacher lead to get defensive about the evidence people share and to fixate on trying to explain and justify what happened. One way to address this proactively is to make it a norm that when discussing classroom evidence we use the word "teacher" rather than the teacher's name. For example, "When the teacher leaned in to listen, the students who hadn't been speaking began to talk."

It can feel a little stiff at first to use "the teacher" rather than the person's name, and it helps to acknowledge this. A facilitator might say, for example, "It may feel strange to say 'teacher' when we all know Kathy taught the lesson. Let's still use 'teacher' to use language of shared ownership for our lesson as we talk about what *all of us* as teachers do and can do."

This subtle language shift fosters a sense of shared ownership, and it also helps the team look at one another as they share evidence rather than all looking at Kathy and saying "you" or Kathy with each detail shared. Such language is especially valuable when evidence in a lesson indicates many student challenges. Kathy, especially, is more likely to learn from what wasn't working if she can look at it honestly without feeling that her peers attribute the challenges to her.

STEP 2: ORGANIZE DATA

After we share our observations, our next goal is to make sense of the data. We look at the evidence and organize it in ways that will help us make generalizations. We put similar data together in clusters or categories, then make generalizations from the data that one team member

Figure 7.1   One Example of How a Team Organized Shared Evidence From a Lesson

writes on the board. In this open-ended sorting task, there are many possible ways teams might group data. There is no right answer. What matters is the team takes time with the data to look for patterns relevant to the POP, and comes up with generalizations that will drive the next step of the process.

1. Silently reread the different details on self-stick notes and think of how to group similar data.

2. Collaborate to cluster the notes into groups or categories that illuminate trends.

Tips

- Group evidence in ways that help you answer team inquiry questions.
- Not all data connect. A piece of evidence may be its own category. Welcome this!
- Be open to diverse perspectives in how to organize the data. This is an open-ended task, and the organization is less important than the insights. If helpful, begin the next step of writing generalizations while organizing to capture all ideas.

Video Example

Scan the following QR code to access the video:

Reflect on the Video

- What are participants doing in the video?
- The facilitator on the far right, Tonya, stands back at first. How does this impact the conversation?
- When does she step in and why? How does this impact the conversation?
- Would you facilitate in a similar or different way? Why?

Facilitator Questions/Prompts

- How can we organize these data to help us make sense of them?
- Which pieces of data might be grouped together?
- What similarities do you see?
- What patterns do you notice?

Possible Challenges and Solutions for Facilitators

Challenge: People stare at the data without suggesting groupings.

Try one or more of the following:

- Provide think time.
- Acknowledge this is an open-ended task without a right answer.
- Model clustering data using "think aloud." For example, "I notice there are many different pieces of evidence about partner interaction. We could cluster those together in a category about how partners interact. Does that make sense?" If others agree, move evidence about partner interactions into one cluster and label the cluster "partner interaction." If not, ask for other ideas for how to group the data. Model with an idea someone shares.
- Pick up a piece of evidence and read it aloud. Ask, "Is there other data that relates to this?" Encourage team members to read and find it; create and name a category together.

Challenge: There is disagreement about how to group the data.

Try one or more of the following:

- Acknowledge this is an open-ended task without a right answer—there are many different ways we might cluster the data.
- Take time to listen. Value each person's unique way of looking at the data and learn from what they have to say.
- Encourage the use of subcategories to incorporate different angles. For example, if one person wants to cluster evidence related to partner interactions and another wants to group together the evidence of students justifying ideas in conversation, create a large group of partner interaction data and subgroups within that data including "justifying ideas."
- Value productive debate as it helps deepen understandings of the data. Remember that deciding how to group the data is less important than the meaning we make from them together. Rather

than trying to come to agreement about the grouping, take time to cluster data in the different ways people recommend and make generalizations about the data from each point of view.

Be Open to the Unexpected

There are times when a team conversation builds in ways we don't expect, and what people are saying seems like a detour from the protocol step. As a facilitator, in those moments, I always ask myself, "Is this conversation deepening team learning? Is it driving team inquiry in a way that is safe for all participants?" If yes, I do not step in. Instead, I listen to how it unfolds, and take notes to remember insights shared so we can connect back to them when they relate to next steps in the protocol: making generalizations, linking cause and effect, or planning.

The most common place for this to happen is when we are organizing data. The conversation naturally elicits statements of generalization: "Most students can . . ." or "Many . . ." This is good, as making generalizations is the next step and the reason we organize data. If it doesn't disrupt the flow of the conversation, it can help to have one team member start writing the generalization statements people share on the board. If that disrupts the conversation, another approach is to jot down the generalizations silently as you hear them. Then, when you move to the official "brainstorm generalizations" step of the protocol, acknowledge the team already came up some generalizations as they were clustering data and read them aloud for the team scribe to write on the board.

STEP 3: MAKE GENERALIZATIONS

After clustering the data to look for trends, we write trends in the form of generalizations. Our generalizations are statements the team agrees to be true based on the evidence we observed. We identify and agree on these one by one as a team and write them down for three primary reasons:

- To make sense of the many separate pieces of evidence
- To come to agreement about what the data show us
- To write down key ideas we'll use to drive the next step of our collaboration

A generalization is an interpretation of data. In this step, we move beyond simply describing to engage in a form of collective interpretation.

After helping teams effectively describe without judgment, it is important to emphasize that description is only the first step of a protocol that evolves from low-level thinking and low depth of knowledge tasks to high-level thinking and high depth of knowledge tasks. We build from describing to identifying patterns and summarizing in these first steps, and next, we engage in drawing conclusions, analyzing, and creating.

It's okay to interpret at this stage, as long as we keep our focus on summarizing key trends in the data—not on evaluating what these trends mean. Generalize what the students said and/or did. For example, "Given the opportunity to speak to a partner before writing, most students started writing. Few talked with a partner first." Notice the focus is on students and their actions. The only interpretation involved in this statement is the word choice for the quantifying adjective, such as "most" or "few." We don't want to make a generalization that includes additional interpretations. Compare these statements:

"ELLs were silent in the conversation."

"ELLs can't talk with partners."

Which is a generalization of evidence? Which is an interpretation of what it means? Which is more specific about what the team observed in one lesson?

As a general rule, try to replace statements about student capacity (can't, can, are able to) with statements focused on a moment in time (did, didn't, were). This language is consistent with a growth mindset (Dweck, 2008) that no matter what students struggle with now, they have capacity to learn and do more.

Protocol Directions

1. Make generalizations from the data about student actions, understandings, and confusions demonstrated in the lesson.

2. Choose a team member to write generalization statement on the board or chart paper.

Tips

Use qualifiers like *few*, *some*, or *all* to align generalizations to how many students participate in the lesson tasks. For example

"Few students..." "Some students..." "Most students..." "All students..."

"2/20 students..." "No girls..." "When asked to _____, most students..."

Video Example

Scan the following QR code to access the video:

Reflect on the Video

- Who suggests each generalization: participants or the facilitator (Tonya on the right)?
- How do participants collaborate to confirm or revise a generalization? What evidence do they discuss to determine if the statement should begin with "most" or "all?"
- Why does the facilitator encourage the team to generalize without using the word "successful?" How do they revise the generalization to describe without evaluation?
- What would you say or do differently if you were facilitating this team discussion?

Facilitator Questions/Prompts

- What generalizations can we make from these data?
- After one person suggests a generalization, ask others, "Based on what you observed, would you agree? Is that statement consistent with what you observed?"
- Would this statement be true for some, most, or all? How many students did each of us see do/say _____? Compare lesson notes to come to agreement on approximately how many students each generalization represents (all, most, some, few, two out of four, etc.).

TEACH AND PRACTICE THE PROTOCOL

Workshop Activity: Introduce and Practice Protocol With a Video

What? Teachers take notes during a five- to seven-minute video to practice describing without judgment and to gather notes they will use to engage in a simulated debrief.

When? Use this activity following the observation practice activity detailed in Chapter 6, and ideally with an extension of the same video. See the launch workshop agenda in Appendix A for recommendations on how to integrate all activities in this book into a cohesive workshop.

Time: 50–70 minutes

Materials

- One copy of *Appendix B: Easy Protocol Reference* for each participant
- Green note cards, on which each participant has written, "What's the evidence?" (City, Elmore, Fiarman, & Teitel, 2009)
- Paper or laptops/tablets for taking notes.
- A 5- to 10-minute video of classroom instruction in which the camera focuses on students talking, writing, or responding rather than simply listening to a teacher. For continuity, consider using a longer section of the same video you used for the observation activity in Chapter 6.

Procedure

1. Briefly introduce the steps of the protocol using *Appendix B: Easy Protocol Reference,* and explain that we will observe a short video from a lesson both to practice taking notes and to engage in a simulation of a lesson debrief discussion.

2. Confirm all are ready to get started. Remind observers to be specific in describing what students are saying and doing. Show the video clip.

3. After the video, use *Appendix B: Easy Protocol Reference* to guide participants through the debrief process. Lead the full process for describe, analyze, and make generalizations.

4. The last protocol step, Link Cause and Effect, which is the focus of the next chapter, is best to experience in the process of analyzing a live lesson the team has planned. In this simulation activity, you may choose to omit this step or briefly practice it by discussing ways to address one generalization. Read Chapter 8 for specifics on the final protocol step including video examples you can use to first introduce it to teams.

REFLECTION QUESTIONS

- How is the OI protocol similar to approaches you use or have tried? How is it different?
- When you next observe and discuss a lesson with colleagues, will you use these protocol steps, revise them, or use a different approach? Explain.

- What steps will you take to build the capacity of colleagues to discuss observation data together?
- How will you engage teams in comfortably gathering and sharing not just the "nice" data of what is working, but also evidence that illuminates challenges and opportunities for growth?

8 From Observation to Action

"There is already a shift in how teachers are using their planning time together. There is less of a focus on just planning and more on reflecting on student learning and refining instruction to meet their needs."

—Maureen Rudder, Principal
McDowell Elementary, Petaluma City Schools

Looking at data and making generalizations often lead teachers to have "aha" insights about how instructional actions impact student learning. Those insights, however, are held in the minds of individuals until teams elicit and explore them collaboratively with the forth protocol step: link cause and effect.

This is when the conversation moves from an analysis of student data to direct reflection on instructional choices to connect the dots between how students learn and what we can do to meet their needs. Identifying and shaping the causal links between teaching and learning is the primary goal of observation inquiry (OI). The more attuned we become to how our teaching actions impact student outcomes, the more skilled we become at shifting those actions in response to student successes and challenges to reach every child.

From Observation to Action

In this part of the debrief protocol, teams build from analyzing data (Steps 1–3) to determining specifically what they can do with the data to shift teaching and student learning (Steps 4–6).

1. Describe

2. Organize data

3. Make generalizations

4. Link cause and effect

5. Apply learning to plan

6. Set individual and team goals

Notice that in Steps 4–6 we shift from being observers to being agents of change. In this chapter, we will explore each collaborative step with an emphasis on the questions, strategies, and in-the-moment decisions we use to facilitate deep discussions.

STEP 4: LINK CAUSE AND EFFECT

Imagine the team has just finished describing and organizing data, then making generalizations from the data. The teams now look together at a list of generalizations they have created from the data, such as a following example generated by a first-grade team in a primarily ELL school after a lesson on story retelling:

- Many students retold using specific adjectives from the story and their own knowledge.
- Many volunteered to add adjectives or details to what their partner shared.
- Pair-share participation increased when the teacher was close to pairs.
- Wait time and questioning increased student responses.
- Some students didn't participate in partner conversations.
- Every student who reported to the whole class gave relevant story details.
- When asked a higher order-thinking question, some students retold story details instead of the task. Some students expressed and justified an opinion.

Now what? How does a team leverage insights from this one lesson to deepen our collaboration and learning? How do we learn from this data together in ways that strengthens our teaching?

A simple and powerful way to structure this part of the conversation involves three steps:

1. Prioritize what to discuss.

2. Celebrate successes.

3. Address challenges.

Prioritize What to Discuss

Have each team member star up to three generalizations that are their top priorities to discuss as a team. Begin with the items that have stars, and address the others only if there is time and team interest.

Why prioritize?

- Save time by focusing on what matters most.
- Foster teacher ownership and choice.
- Sharpen the collective focus to the next edge of learning for students and teachers.

Time: 2–3 minutes

The team reads over the list of generalizations generated together from the lesson. Each person draws a star next to one to three priorities they wish to discuss together.

It helps to introduce this step by explaining the purpose within the big picture of what will follow. For example, "We will next discuss some of these generalizations to illuminate together actions that have led to student successes and ways we can address challenges together. To maximize our time together, let's identify which generalizations are our top priorities to discuss."

Facilitator Prompts/Questions

- Which of the generalizations listed are your top priorities to discuss?
- Which would you like to have an opportunity to discuss in depth as a team?
- Draw a star by one to two that is either an outcome you want to achieve in your classroom or a challenge you want to collaborate to address.

Teachers typically will put stars by generalizations that are opportunities for teacher learning, including student struggles or challenges in how they respond. In this first-grade example earlier, teachers each prioritized the same two generalizations:

- Some students didn't participate in partner conversations.
- When asked a higher order-thinking question, some students retold story details instead of the task. Some students expressed and justified an opinion.

Such consensus is helpful, but not essential. Often, stars are widely distributed and reveal a range of two to five priorities to discuss.

Nimble Facilitation Moves

- If there are fewer than five generalizations and time to discuss each, skip this step.
- If time is limited for the discussion, have each person star only one priority.
- If the stars people draw are spread out across many generalizations, and if there is only time to discuss some, then ask the teacher who taught the lesson which generalization he or she would like to discuss first. Have each team member in turn choose a starred item from the list.

Two Ways to Link Cause and Effect

The team then discusses each starred priority to identify the instructional actions that have led to or could lead to the desired result. We approach the conversation in one of two ways, depending on the generalization:

- Celebrate: When it is a generalization the team wishes to replicate, such as a student success, the team identifies actions that *lead to* this student outcome.
- Address challenges: If it is a challenge, the team collaborates to brainstorm the specific instructional actions and opportunities they *anticipate will help* students succeed with this challenge.

These two conversations are similar in that both focus on the cause-and-effect connections between teaching and learning. We collaborate to identify specific instructional actions that we can take to enhance student learning relevant to our team goals. The subtle, but important difference is that with a success, we highlight the strategies we want to *continue using* to realize the *same* result, and with a challenge, we focus on strategies we can *add or revise* to realize a *different* result.

Before I detail how we celebrate successes and address challenges, I want to emphasize an important point: these are not always distinct steps. Often we discuss a generalization as both a success and a challenge. Many outcomes in a classroom involve a combination of both, especially when teams focus on equity. For example, imagine a team has starred this generalization to discuss: "Some students point to the text and cite specific text evidence when justifying their ideas to a partner." The success to replicate is the outcome: students are citing text evidence to justify ideas. The challenge to address is the adjective: some. In our debrief as we brainstorm ways we can engage *all* students in citing text evidence to justify ideas, we discuss both the strategies we know are working for some students and the strategies we can add or refine to help *all* students excel with the goal.

Think of the protocols for discussing successes and challenges as tools for your facilitation tool-kit, not a script. The better you understand the merits and nuances of each, the more prepared you are to lead teams in deep conversations: no matter how the lesson goes or what the student data reveals.

Link Cause and Effect: Celebrate Successes

Why celebrate successes?

- Affirm our collective impact on student learning
- Highlight specific strategies to use again
- Celebrate short-term wins to fuel the team (Kotter, 2012)
- Facilitate a sharing of expertise within the team

Time: 5–10 minutes

The team identifies a generalization they want to replicate (e.g., all students referred to the text in the discussion) and infers together the instructional actions that led to this student outcome. Teachers discuss both strategies within the observed lesson and ask the lead teacher to share strategies used before the lesson that could have led to this ultimate result. One team member takes notes to share with the team using the note-taking template from Figure 8.1 Note-Taking Template: Link Cause and Effect, or a similar format to take notes digitally.

Video Example

In this video, a middle school team discusses a lesson outcome they want to replicate across all classrooms. Notice how teachers build from talking about what led students to this success within this one lesson, to how to take students to the next level of learning from this point.

Scan the following QR code to access the video:

During this conversation, the facilitator used the same format as Figure 8.2 to type these digital notes for the team:

Generalization: All students used their books and teaching to complete note-taking tasks throughout the lesson.
Instructional actions that can lead them to this success:

- Clear expectations to take notes
- Note-taking scaffold
- Materials are prepared and ready to use
- Have students read headers to predict text structure and create a framework for note-taking
- Build from a scaffold to student independence with note-taking
- Collaborate as a staff to build a shared progression of expectations across all grades

Facilitator Questions and Prompts

- When looking at a generalization to discuss, ask, "Is this a generalization we want to replicate?" If teachers agree it is, use the following questions. If not, use questions from the next section for addressing a challenge.
- Clarify what you are doing and why. For example, "Let's take a celebration moment to reflect on how we got students to this point and identify what actions we can take in the future to realize the same result."
- Ask questions to generate an open brainstorm about cause and effect. Follow the brainstorm with debate and discussion. Here are some examples of questions to generate thinking about cause and effect:
  - o What instructional actions do we believe led to this outcome for students? What did we observe within this lesson? What did students experience before this lesson that could help them realize this outcome?
  - o In a new class with different students, what actions can we take as teachers to realize the same results?

Figure 8.1

Note-Taking Template: Link Cause and Effect

Team: _____ Date:_____

1. Write a generalization that is a priority to discuss:

   _____

   _____

2. Write instructional actions and opportunities that will help students excel in this area. If they are already excelling, identify the ways to repeat this success with other students in other classrooms. If the generalization reflects a challenge, brainstorm solutions. Write all possible actions and opportunities the team brainstorms here:

3. Identify idea(s) to incorporate into the next team-planned lesson. Write a star next to these prioritized idea(s), and then use these notes as a reminder when planning the next lesson together.

Skip This Step Based on Team Priorities

If there are no successes represented in the generalizations, skip this step. Depending on the data gathered and the priorities selected by the team, there may not be a conversation about successes. This is okay. This does not indicate the absence of success, only a collective focus on challenges in our observation data. Often, teams take the successes in stride and want to focus their precious collaboration time on the challenges: the edge of new learning. When all starred priorities are challenges, be nimble with the protocol and go right into discussing the generalizations the team has prioritized.

Add This Step to Illuminate Team Learning

When a team doesn't prioritize a success to discuss, a nimble facilitator will often follow their lead to go straight into discussing the challenges. There are other times, however, when we see a success in the list of generalizations that we want to make sure doesn't get lost in the shuffle. It can be valuable to take a celebration moment to point out the generalization and identify together what specifically led to that outcome. This is especially important if a success realized in the lesson may not yet be realized across all classrooms represented by the teacher team. In such cases, even when the team did not star a success as a priority, a nimble facilitator may choose to briefly "take a celebration moment" to read the generalization about student learning aloud and engage the team in illuminating what led to that result. This will reinforce the learning, help all team members identify specifically how to apply it to their classrooms, and also prepare the team with specific notes on their effective practices they can share with other colleagues beyond the team.

Link Cause and Effect: Address Challenges

After discussing generalizations we want to replicate, we delve into the challenges.
Why?

- Shift the conversation from what we observed to what specifically we can do.
- Share expertise to collectively refine instruction.
- Maximize our impact by using data to get specific about challenges: the next edge of learning for our students and ourselves.

The team rereads the generalizations they have prioritized that represent a student challenge. For each, they brainstorm and discuss instructional actions they can take to address this challenge in future lessons across all team classrooms. Similar to the approach with successes, one member takes note in a digital format or with the note-taking template in Figure 8.1.

Facilitation Questions/Prompts

- What is a challenge we want to address together?
- What specific strategies/modeling/lessons do we anticipate will help all learners succeed with this challenge?
- What additional questions do we have about addressing this challenge?
- What are resources (texts, people, online) we could access to help us learn more about ways to address this challenge?

Video Example

In the following video, a first-grade team at a Title I school discusses together a generalization from the fifth lesson the team has planned, observed, and analyzed in a year. The team's problem of practice (POP) is "When discussing stories using reading strategies, students are challenged to respond orally to partners. Many ELLs are reluctant and insecure when speaking about academic content."

When they started OI in the fall, all teachers on the team were new to structuring partner interaction in the classroom. By this point in their process, they have realized success engaging ELLs at all levels in daily conversations about texts, and they are focusing in on a more specific challenge about how students talk beyond a disagreement. The generalization from this lesson observation they discuss in this video is "Some students were able to explain why they disagreed."

Notice how teachers both hypothesize solutions and share classroom experiences in this discussion.

Scan the following QR code to access the video:

Reflect on the Video

- Would this conversation help teachers address this challenge in their classroom? Why or why not?
- Are recommendations shared in this conversation focused toward one teacher or all teachers? Does this matter? Why?

- What role does the facilitator (far right) have in this conversation? If you were the facilitator, what would you ask, say, or do?
- If you were taking notes of ideas for instructional actions or opportunities to take away from this conversation, what would you write?

Nimble Facilitation Moves

Get as Specific as Possible About Challenges

When discussing how students struggle in a lesson, specificity is essential to inform teaching. Our surface data will tell us what students didn't do or what they did wrong. In looking at a challenge, ask questions to help the team get as specific as possible about why they struggle. The goal isn't to identify causal factors beyond the control of a school, but to get specific about the following:

- How students are thinking
- What they seem to understand
- How they approach learning
- How they respond to shifts in instruction

For example, in looking at the generalization, "Some students did not participate in partner discussions," we might ask,

- Did those students talk during any part of the lesson or in other lessons in the past? In what contexts did they participate? What were the specifics of those contexts in terms of the task, the modeling, and interaction with others?

In another example, a fourth-grade team discussed the challenge, "Half of the students wrote the inference on the wrong part of the graphic organizer." To get specific about the issue, they discussed questions including the following:

- What did students write? What can we understand about their thinking process based on what they wrote?
- In watching students during the lesson, what did we notice about their thinking as they used the organizer? What did they write first? What did they write next?
- Was the challenge only with the organizer? Did they make a clear inference and justify it with evidence in their speaking and writing?

These questions helped the team realize the challenge was not simply that students didn't correctly use the organizer. It was that the structure of the organizer that was a distraction from the way students approached the task. Students were writing the inference first, and the organizer was designed with the assumption they'd do the opposite: write text details and prior knowledge before coming up with an inference. The scaffold was confusing them, not the task itself.

Understanding the problem is essential to identifying solutions. If we'd stopped at "they did it wrong," we might have simply identified modeling and guided practice as the solution. By delving deeper, we learned we needed to shift our approach to scaffolding the task.

Be Intentional With Verb Tense

Notice a key distinction in how we link instruction to successes versus challenges. For a success, we look backward and ask, "What instructional actions do we infer led to this success?"

For a challenge, we look forward and ask, "What instructional moves do we anticipate will help students excel with this challenge?"

Why is it important to focus toward the future when discussing student-learning challenges as a team? Benefits include safety, shared ownership, and a forward-focus toward collective action.

Consider the following shifts in language for framing a recommendation after a lesson observation. How might the way we frame a recommendation impact how others hear it? Which of the following starters for sharing feedback are more likely to foster safety, shared ownership, and collective action?

Past Focus on Individual Actions	Forward Focus for Collective Action
I would have done . . . You should have . . .	To address this we can . . . In the next lesson let's . . . One way to address this challenge is . . . We can help students succeed with this challenge by . . .

Use Pronouns for Collective Responsibility

Notice the starters in the previous table include not only future tense, but also pronouns for collective responsibility. Using "we" or "us" helps bring all observers into the driver's seat as agents of change. Compare the following two approaches to inviting a team to brainstorm ways to address a challenge:

A. "One challenge prioritized to discuss is 'Some students didn't participate in the pair-share. What could Amy (the teacher lead) have done differently to address this challenge?"

B. "One challenge you prioritized to discuss is 'Some students didn't participate in the pair-share'. Is this a challenge we are experiencing in our classrooms? What can we do as teachers to engage the students who don't participate? What strategies will help us address this challenge in all of our classrooms?"

Reflect: How are these two approaches similar? How are they different? Which would you use? Why? Which approach best helps participants connect the conversation to their practice? Why?

Using collective pronouns (we, our, us) as in Approach A has two primary benefits: (1) It builds safety for the teacher lead to take risks, make mistakes, and never be the target of collective critique, and (2) it fosters collective responsibility for team members to own the challenge and address it across all classrooms. There is no one in the room who is simply an observer. We are participating and reflecting as agents of change.

Redirect Feedback

Sometimes at this stage of the debrief people begin focusing on the teacher who taught the lesson and offering direct feedback. This is not always a bad thing, and it is encouraged in some lesson study protocols. It can be problematic in a group setting if one of the following occurs:

- Feedback is based on debatable opinions.
- The teacher receiving feedback gets defensive.
- Collaborators maintain an external focus (on how to help a colleague), rather than reflect on how to change their practice.

Sometimes the teacher who teaches the lesson will ask for feedback from their peers. In these cases, it often works well to make an exception to the protocol as the teacher has requested the feedback and is ready to hear what colleagues say. Specific questions about parts of the lesson or student challenges solicit specific feedback, the most helpful kind for learning. By contrast, general questions such as, "What did you think?" can often lead to general pat-on-the-back statements such as, "You were great!" that feed the ego but not learning.

Aside from the times a teacher asks for specific feedback, it is productive to keep to the protocol of avoiding "you" statements directed at the teacher who taught the lesson. This doesn't mean a team should avoid all suggestions and recommendations. In fact, such reflection and insights are a priority at this stage. The difference is with language: Instead of using "you" use "we." Instead of "should" or "should have" ask questions using "I wonder."

Here are some examples of directed feedback and alternatives that invite collective reflection and change:

Feedback Directed at One Teacher	Invitations for Collective Reflection
You could have . . .? You should have . . . ? Why didn't you . . . ?	"I wonder how students would respond if we . . ." What will happen if we try . . ." We could . . .

Avoiding direct feedback is not the same as avoiding feedback all together. In essence, the debrief protocol is all about feedback. It's just not framed as "feedback." It's not personal and it's not evaluative, but it is the most informative feedback there is: evidence of student understanding or misunderstanding, evidence of student participation or passivity, evidence of student thinking. It is precise, formative feedback that helps a team understand what learning is and is not happening during instruction. It helps teachers reflect on the specific cause-and-effect relationships between instructional actions and student learning. We don't call it feedback because we are very intentionally steering clear of having every team member share opinions on what the teacher lead could do differently. That said, the discussion protocol intentionally integrates the elements of effective feedback highlighted in research (Thurlings, Vermeulen, Kreijns, Bastiaens, & Stijen, 2012) including the following:

- A focus on student learning
- Goal-driven
- Constructive via detailed talk about observations
- Balanced with emphasis on successes and challenges

Consider how these elements of effective feedback are built into the OI protocols for discussing lessons. For deeper analysis on the role of feedback in OI, reflect also on the following questions:

- How are the elements of effective feedback built into the OI protocols for discussing lessons?
- What are advantages and disadvantages of having peers provide direct feedback to individual teachers in a team setting?
- Imagine an observer makes a direct recommendation to the teacher lead, and the teacher gets defensive. As a facilitator, how would you address this?

Expand the Frame of Reference

One facilitation strategy is to ask questions that help a team reframe a problem or situation to see it in a new way. Focusing on the details of student learning within one lesson is like using the zoom function on a camera. From data gathering, to generalizations and cause-and-effect interpretations, the team narrows their focus into the specific details of a slice of instructional time.

This narrow focus has many benefits in helping a team understand students and the impact of instructional moves. It can also be limiting, especially when students succeed in a lesson, yet not with the end goal. In these cases, a team might focus only on how to replicate the successes without also looking forward to the next level of learning.

For example, a fourth-grade team focusing on helping students identify key details in a text taught a lesson in which most students were successful. As most generalizations reflected an outcome the teachers wanted to replicate, their debrief discussion centered on instructional strategies they had used and would continue to use. It was a celebratory discussion, confirming what the team had learned could work to achieve these same results again.

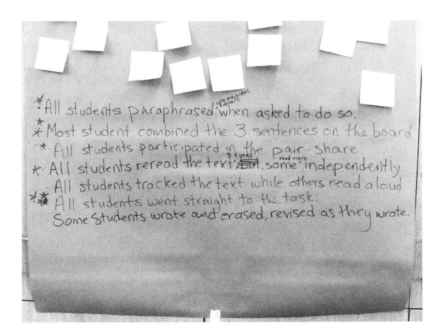

Celebrating successes is important, and yet the conversation should not stop there—especially when students are far from excelling with the end-of-year goal. The facilitator asked the team three important questions to deepen the discussion:

1. What is the end task we wish students to do to demonstrate success with our POP?

2. How is the task in today's lesson similar or different?

3. What is the next level of learning for students to excel with the *end task/goal*?

The first question reframed the lesson outcomes into a larger context: the end goal for excelling with the team's POP. The second question asked the team to get specific about the modeling, scaffolds, and supports within this lesson and how they compared to the final assessment task. In this conversation, the team identified the following:

Today's Lesson	End-of-Year Goal
Teacher reads text aloud first.	Students read text independently.
Students' reread with partners, then independently.	Across a multiple paragraph text, students identify and paraphrase key details independently.
In individual paragraphs, students identify key details and paraphrase them to a partner.	

In comparing the lesson to the end goal, the team expanded their frame of reference from the lesson to the larger end goal. This helped them identify the next level of learning for students and themselves. A big-picture view is critical especially in schools where students traditionally underperform, as it can be easy-to-use logic such as the following:

When we provide heavy scaffolds, our diverse learners are successful. Thus, we must provide heavy scaffolds to ensure our diverse learners succeed.

There is some truth to this statement, especially when we only look at the evidence within one lesson. It is also missing an important element: release of responsibility. While celebrating the gains our students make in a context of scaffolds and modeling, we must always look ahead to the goal beyond the scaffolds and intentionally plan a path toward increased task complexity and student independence. Reframing a success into the context of a bigger challenge to solve helps teams build on what is working to continuously raise the bar.

STEP 5: APPLY LEARNING TO PLAN

After discussing generalizations from the lesson data and identifying specific ways to build on successes and address challenges, OI teams collaborate to apply what they have learned to plan the next lesson.

There are different ways for teams to apply learning to plan the next lesson including refining, redesigning, refocusing, and raising rigor. In Chapter 9, we'll explore the nuances of how teams build from one lesson to plan the next and what facilitators can do to support the process. In the meantime, here are general questions to consider in planning a subsequent lesson:

Logistics

- Who will teach the lesson?
- When will it be?
- Who will cover classes?

Learning Progressions

- Where are students now on a progression of learning toward our goal?
- What will we teach between now and the next lesson? Where do we anticipate they will be on the next date for our lesson inquiry?
- Build from this expectation to draft a plan, and then revisit the specifics of scaffolding and modeling within a week of the lesson. It is ideal to schedule a team meeting at that time, if possible, so the teacher lead is not alone making the final adjustments.

Content Context

- What will be the instructional context for the lesson? At that time, where will students be in the curriculum, and what connections to that specific content will we make? If our lesson involves reading, what text will be most relevant to use?

Strategies

- Which of the strategies we discussed today do we want to incorporate into our next lesson? Consider both what we will continue doing to realize similar results and what we will change, refine, or test to realize different results. What student successes will we build on? What challenges that we observed today do we want to address?

Observation Focus

- If the lesson involves a series of elements, which will be most essential to observe together? Which will provide the most formative data about student learning and the impact of our instructional moves?
- What will be our observation priorities in the lesson? Revisit focus questions.

STEP 6: SET INDIVIDUAL AND TEAM GOALS

Wrap up each team collaboration with time for personal reflection and goal setting.

Why?

- Foster reflective practice
- Support the transfer of learning to practice
- Engage teachers in shaping their own learning

Time: 5–10 minutes

1. The facilitator poses the question, "Of everything we've observed and discussed today, what specifically do you want to take from this experience to apply to your own teaching?" Set one or two goals that you want to focus on in the next several weeks before we meet again.

2. All team members including the facilitator write goals, either on a digital file they can access at each meeting or on a copy of Figure 8.2 Individual Goals/Plans for Action (located at the end of this chapter).

3. Team members each take a turn sharing their goals.

From individual goals, then reflect on the question: "Are there any team goals we want to set or agreements we want to make as a result of our learning today?"

When all teachers agree on a shared goal, write it on a shared digital file or copy of Figure 8.3 Team Agreements/Plans for Action (located at the end of this chapter).

It's not necessary to set team agreements, and it doesn't happen each time, but often there is a rich opportunity to agree as a team on a practice they all want to try to support one another in using. A team agreement can lead to instructional consistencies that will benefit students such as the following examples:

Opening Doors to Equity

- A cross-disciplinary middle school team agreed to a standard proto-col to use Cornell notes.
- A multigrade elementary team agreed to use the same categories and visual chart for teaching students discourse moves.

These consistencies help students by facilitating connections across learn-ing contexts and supporting routines that help students move more easily toward independent success. Consistent tools or routines across a site help teachers move instruction from the teaching of procedures to the use of procedures for deeper learning.

Team agreements also benefit teachers. When teachers all agree to use a common strategy or focus on a common goal, they can support one in continuous planning, reflection, and idea sharing relevant to that goal. For example, when a fourth-grade team made a team agreement to teach character-trait adjectives to support ELLs with literary analysis, they then followed up with one another to identify words to teach, compare word banks, and share their successes and challenges implementing strategies on their own.

Nimble Facilitation Moves

- If many share the same goal, ask, "Is this a goal we want to consider setting together as a team? Should we make this a team agreement so we can then all support one another with ideas and reflect together on how it is working?"
- If there is a team agreement, have all write it. If there isn't, don't force it. There are plenty of next steps for all to focus on already with individual goals and the next team lesson in the next cycle of inquiry.

Plan to reflect together on team and individual goals at the start of the next team meeting. Make time to share ideas, success, and challenges with these goals before delving into the next lesson for inquiry.

REFLECTION QUESTIONS

- How will you engage teachers in making cause-and-effect links between instructional actions and student learning? What challenges do you anticipate? How will you address these challenges?
- When you set a goal, what systems or supports help you realize it?
- What systems and supports will you use to help colleagues set goals, reflect on goals, and realize them in their teaching practice?

Figure 8.2 Individual Goals/Plans for Action

Date	My Goal/ Plan for Action	Notes

learning progressions across the year. One teacher reflected, "A process like this has forced me to be hands on . . . and do the follow-through and not put it off. Meeting, knowing we were going to do this, helped me with specific skills."

The team **refined** their approach in these specific ways:

- Increased structure for partner interactions: model expectations, assign roles for turn-taking, knee to knee, silent think time with thumb up when ready to share
- Adjusted timing to keep lessons to fewer than 20 minutes
- Integrated movement into every read aloud
- Provided language scaffolds specific to each task

Examples of how they raised **rigor** include the following:

- Continual elevation of expectations from hoping students would participate in pair-share, to expecting all students to respond using complete sentences and text evidence to justify their thinking
- From talking about the topic of texts to discussing text evidence
- From low depth of knowledge to higher depth of knowledge tasks
- From talking to writing
- From simple to complex texts
- From familiar to academic contexts
- From informal to formal language

The team also **released responsibility** by moving from guiding conversations with rehearsal and scaffolds to facilitating student-led interactions.

Shifts in Teacher Practice

The multilesson progression helps teachers make a difference for students and deepen their own learning. Notice, for example, how in this kindergarten/first-grade team teachers' individual reflections and goals evolved across the year:

Lesson Dates	Goals Individual Teachers Set
October	Structure partner conversations rather than calling on individuals.
December	Increase student participation in partner conversations. Create more opportunities for students to talk about texts. Incorporate movement in lessons.

Lesson Dates	Goals Individual Teachers Set
January	Ask more text-dependent questions. Teach students to justify thinking within partner conversations. Model expected language use and support with frames.
February	Refine timing of pair-share tasks within a lesson. Incorporate physical responses, choral responses, and think-pair-share opportunities into all read alouds. Make the use of these strategies a natural part of how I teach every day.

From October through February, via four half-days of collaborative professional learning, teachers moved from trying partner conversations for the first time to integrating them strategically into a read aloud routine to elevate student participation, language use, and thinking about texts. Compare this outcome to the impact of sit-and-get trainings in the same district in the previous year: Teachers had developed an understanding of strategies, but did not use them. By contrast, within 12 hours of team inquiry around live lessons, the team transformed their daily teaching.

Reflect

- What shifts did the team realize in student learning and participation?
- What shifts did teachers make in their practice?
- What do you anticipate would be the next level of learning for this team?

SECOND GRADE: DEEPENING INSIGHTS ABOUT LANGUAGE

McDowell Elementary School, Petaluma City Schools

Demographics

- 286 students
- 95.8% qualify for free or reduced price meals
- 79.1% ELL
- 2.4% African American, 2.7% Asian, 0.7% Filipino, 86% Hispanic/Latino, 7.5% white

POP: Based on assessment data, we choose, students are not making sense of multiple meaning words within the context of their reading.

Inquiry Questions

> o Do student use vocabulary strategies while reading?
> o How are students checking for understanding?

Lesson 1: The team planned the first lesson to teach the concept of multiple meaning words via instruction of one word with multiple meanings. The lesson involved these key features:

- Teach three meanings of the word using a circle map, images, and text.
- Engage students in using the different meanings in structured partner discussions.
- Have students collaborate with a partner to read sentences and match each to the correct meaning of the word.

In this first structured lesson, the majority of students demonstrated an understanding of multiple meanings by correctly matching sentences to definitions. Few collaborated in the partner task, however. In most cases, one student did the work as the other silently watched.

Lesson 2*:* Building from these data, teachers planned a second lesson involving a new multiple-meaning word. They used a similar approach but **refined** the partner task to make it more interactive and, specifically, to engage students in justifying their thinking during the collaboration. In their observation data, teachers noted that student participation, language use, and understandings increased in this second lesson.

Lesson 3: In planning for Lesson 3, it would have been easy to repeat the success of that lesson by refining small details and repeating the lesson in a new context. The facilitator saw an opportunity, however, for the deeper student and teacher learning. She used the strategy of expanding the frame of reference detailed in the previous chapter by asking

1. What is the end task we wish students do to demonstrate success with our POP?
2. How is the task in today's lesson similar or different?
3. What is the next level of learning for students to excel with the *end* task/goal?

The team revisited the performance task they had created to measure success with the end goal, a task similar in format and content to tasks on the state ELA test students would take in spring. It was more challenging than the tasks in their lesson in complexity, scaffolds, and context. They used a backward design (Wiggins & McTighe, 2005) approach to plan the opportunities needed for students to realize success with the end goal. They collaborated to raise the bar from the first lesson to increase rigor and release responsibility over the course of the next lessons.

This involved not just a refinement of the first lesson that built background for students, but a newly **designed** approach involving a more complex integration of skills, student problem solving, and independence. Teachers determined together the instructional steps students needed to realize the end goal. To achieve this end, they **raised rigor** and **released responsibility** across Lessons 3 and 4.

The following examples are ways the team **increased rigor** across lessons:

- Raised depth of knowledge demands of the tasks
- Increase complexity and length of texts involved
- From targeted instruction to integrated application
- From personal context to academic context

The team also **released responsibility** in these specific ways:

- Reduced modeling
- Reduced scaffolds
- Increase opportunities for student risk taking
- Shifted from teacher lead to student lead

Student learning gains: After the final lesson in March, the team reflected back on the shifts in student learning since September.

September	March
• Most students could not perform assessment tasks of matching a sentence to a different sentence that uses the same meaning of the word. • They could not complete the task even when the teacher read all sentences aloud.	• All performed the grade-level high-stakes assessment tasks without hesitation. • The majority performed three out of four tasks correctly after reading the sentences independently.
• When given a matching and sorting task, most pairs could not complete the task with discussion. Often one partner just grabbed the papers and did the work silently.	• All students worked collaboratively in pair tasks and took turns in an ongoing dialogue. They asked questions, shared ideas, justified, agreed, and/or disagreed.

(Continued)

(Continued)

September	March
• Even if they had the right answer, most students could not justify why they matched the sentence to the meaning.	• All students justified their thinking aloud in peer conversations.
• Teachers were the only ones pointing out multiple-meaning words.	• Across all second-grade classrooms, students demonstrated word consciousness. They were word detectives, finding multiple-meaning words in many contexts outside of vocabulary lessons.

Notice these gains extend beyond the POP emphasis on multiple-meaning words. In building from lesson to lesson, teachers also refined teaching to elevate participation, thinking, and language use. They realized elevated student engagement in partner discourse, and realized gains for all ELLs in the discourse skill of justifying and explaining ideas.

Justification became a major planning focus after the first lesson, when the team observed that few students were able to justify their ideas. In Lesson 2 they provided response frames to support justification and structured opportunities for all students to articulate their ideas.

Deepening Teacher Learning

Observing that lesson and taking notes on what students said as they justified, teachers gained an insight that fueled them to refine their instruction even more. For context, compare these three ways a student tells a partner which meaning of "raise" is being used in the book title *Raising Dragons*:

1. "Meaning Number 1."

2. "I know the title uses the first meaning of raise because it has to do with raise."

3. "I know this book title uses the first meaning of raise because it has to do with taking care of someone from when they are very little until they grow up."

The first is representative of what students said in the first lesson the team planned and observed together. The second represents how most students justified thinking in the second lesson when students referenced a response frame.

Analyzing student quotes from the second lesson together, the team noticed students used the response frame, but didn't actually justify. They simply repeated the vocabulary word in the phrase "It has to do with _____." This "aha" moment helped teachers recognize that to justify thinking about word meanings, students needed more than a sentence frame including "because." They needed vocabulary to paraphrase the meaning of the word without just repeating the word itself. In essence, they needed a deeper understanding of nuances in word meaning and the language to explain it.

With new insights about student abilities and the task demands, the team then collaborated to plan specific ways to help students learn and articulate their thinking at a higher level.

Integrating Language Development

This is one example of how collaborating to pay close attention to observational data helps teachers deepen understanding about the relationships between language, thinking, and content learning. Such understanding is critical for meeting the needs of Academic English Learners, including ELLs, and impossible to develop deeply in workshops that are removed from the context of teaching. As recommended by experts in ELL achievement and professional learning, "Professional development opportunities need to be designed to build the knowledge, strategies and skills of all teachers of ELLs to integrate language development scaffolds for students at varying levels of proficiency within a classroom" (Santos, Darling-Hammond, & Cheuk, 2012, p. 6). OI helps teachers go beyond superficial knowledge to intergrate and apply strategies across diverse contexts to meet the needs of students at varying levels.

Teachers deepen expertise and capacity for building language in academic contexts when they collaborate to

- structure ways for all learners to talk and write about content;
- analyze what students say and write;
- agree on what constitutes an articulate response;
- identify gaps between where students are and the goal;
- plan instruction to address the gap; and
- test and refine approaches until students succeed.

All of these professional learning design features are central to OI and why teams consistently realize deeper understanding of their students and build collective capacity to advance student language use in tandem with content learning goals.

MIDDLE SCHOOL: ELEVATING THINKING ACROSS THE CONTENT AREAS

Mark West Charter School

Demographics

- 169 students
- 33.1% qualify for free and reduced price meals
- 7.7% ELL
- 1.2% American Indian, 2.4% Asian, 1.2% Filipino, 27% Hispanic/ Latino, 62% white

Team: Multidisciplinary Middle School Team: 2 Science Teachers, 2 Social Studies and ELA Teachers, 1 EL Specialist

POP: Students struggle with open-ended speaking and writing tasks requiring high-level thinking. Peer-to-peer talk is especially challenging when students are asked to do more than answer simple questions.

Inquiry Questions

- How do we structure peer interaction so all students participate?
- How can we effectively integrate more high-level thinking tasks into our daily teaching while ensuring diverse learners succeed?

In a multidisciplinary situation, the progression across four lessons usually follows a different path than is typical for a grade-level team focused on one content standard. Rather than building lesson-to-lesson across a learning progression toward a content-specific goal, the team focuses on addressing a global challenge across diverse contexts.

In this charter middle school team, each colleague taught a lesson specific to content learning objectives he or she was teaching at the time. This resulted in a tremendous variation in the content focus of each lesson:

Lesson 1: E's Science Lesson: Structure of an Atom

Lesson 2: C's Science Lesson: Natural Selection

Lesson 3: J's Social Studies Lesson: Comparing Themes Across Chinese Empires

Lesson 4: S's Language Arts Lesson: Charting Plot

Lesson 5: C's Science Lesson: Electromagnetic Waves

Each lesson was different in teacher, students, content area, and grade level. What they shared in common was a focus on structuring peer-to-peer conversations to engage all learners in high-level thinking specific to the lesson goals. The team also intentionally planned the use of academic reading and writing from texts into each lesson to collaborate in testing and refining strategies for building content literacy skills.

At the beginning of the year, structuring partner interactions was a new strategy for most teachers on the team. For the first lesson, they collaborated to plan conversation tasks into a science lesson and then took detailed notes on how pairs interacted. Learning from the successes and challenges, they then **refined** their approach to structuring partner interactions by adding modeling and structures to increase participation.

Across Lessons 2–5, the team collaborated to apply their learning to new lesson contexts. With each lesson, teachers refined their approach to structuring conversation tasks to directly enhance content learning and language development specific to the lesson objectives. Working across diverse contexts is a critical experience for developing this skill, as language and thinking demands vary according to context and task (Schleppegrell, 2004; Fang, Schleppegrell, & Cox, 2006). Across five different lessons in three content areas, teachers identified together the specific ways academic language demands vary by context, and they collaborated to apply the general principal of scaffolding language to specific and varied situations. This shared experience helped them build metaawareness about language and how to support language learning across diverse lessons.

The team **refined** their approach in the following ways:

- Using strategic partnering to build on strengths and address needs
- Aligning discussion tasks to lesson objectives
- Refining the use of reading and Cornell notes to build literacy in tandem with content
- Building routines to help students build metacognition about language and the thinking-level of tasks

The team also **raised rigor** and **released responsibility** via

- elevating the thinking-level demands of tasks;
- reducing scaffolds and structures to foster student initiative and independence; and
- integrating of content literacy into hands-on, interactive tasks.

Deepening Teacher Learning

Specific to their POP, teachers identified gains in how students interacted and discussed high-level thinking tasks. They shifted from frequently calling on individuals to frequently structuring student conversations about lesson content. Through this work, they also identified new questions for inquiry and new opportunities to deepen their work.

One question the team began asking after the first lesson was, "How do we engage students in extended dialogue beyond a simple pair-share?" The team **researched** new strategies by reading the book, *Academic Conversations: Classroom Talk That Fosters Critical Thinking and Content Understandings* (Zwiers & Crawford, 2011), and collaborated to apply what they learned to teaching. Book study in tandem with OI helps teachers both expand their knowledge base and refine the application of knowledge to address the very specific content goals and student needs before them.

The multidisciplinary team built shared understandings about students and instruction together, and through the process made agreements to build shared practices across the grades and content areas of their charter middle school. Their agreements included the following:

- Using three categories of questions in classrooms to build both teachers' and students' metaawareness about thinking in the context of academic tasks
- Supporting diverse learner achievement in content literacy by using strategies including establishing purpose, chunking texts, analysis of vocabulary in context, Cornell notes, and collaborative text-dependent tasks
- Use of peer-to-peer discussions in daily lessons to build language, thinking, and content understandings

By focusing broadly across diverse content areas, this middle school team realized different outcomes than grade-level teams that focused specifically on one content goal. Rather than building across one learning progression for one grade-level goal, they built shared understandings and practices to build coherences in effective instructional practices. They made agreements, and even more important, they became invested in continuing to collaborate across diverse content areas to realize shared goals. They reshaped the culture of collaboration onsite for building academic literacy of all students and ensuring ELL success.

STRATEGIES FOR FACILITATING DEEP LEARNING

In retrospect, the story of how any team learns across lessons is a linear sequence of events. When building from one lesson to plan the next, however, the process is anything but linear. While all three teams described in this chapter share similarities in how they progressed raising rigor, releasing responsibility, and learning together, they are very different in their approach. Their experiences represent three of the ways teams might collaborate across a multilesson inquiry cycle:

1. **Refine an instructional routine.** The kindergarten team refined a routine for engaging all learners, especially ELLs in collaborative conversations about nonfiction texts read aloud. Across different contexts and with different texts, they continued using the same routine and refined it each time.

2. **Build a series of lessons across a learning progression.** The second-grade team first designed and refined a lesson to build foundational understandings, and then planned their third and fourth lesson with new approaches to build from students' prior successes to raise rigor and release responsibility toward the ultimate end goal.

3. **Build shared expertise needed to solve a POP.** The middle school did not refine one instructional routine or build together sequence lessons along a continuum. Through testing and refining strategies across five diverse lessons, they deepened understandings about students' needs and effective instruction specific to their POP and supported one another in applying that learning to diverse contexts.

So which approach will you take when you engage in inquiry across multiple lessons with colleagues? Which approach will you lead when you are in the role of a facilitator? The best answer to this question is the question itself, a mindset that the path you choose will be directed by the goal, your data from the lesson, and how you collaborate to make a bridge between where students are and where they need to be.

Courageous Inquiry

What students say and do in a lesson sometimes surprises us and challenges us to try a new approach. This is especially true when we collaborate at the edge of student learning and our own learning, as we are trying to understand something new or solve what we haven't solved before. Like scientists testing a hypothesis, we may discover our initial assumptions were right or discover there is more to learn, ask, test, and refine. Usually we discover a combination of both: successes to build on and failures that challenge us to think and work in new ways. Do we have the courage to pay attention to data when it challenges us to change how we work? How do we engage in this process together?

A facilitator's primary role is to help the team maintain a mindset of courageous inquiry. This involves both curiosity and flexibility. We don't hang on the means, a set path we expected to follow, such as the goal of refining one lesson approach or building a series of lessons along a learning progression. We commit to asking questions and looking honestly at evidence of student learning and engagement (or confusion and disengagement) to shape how we work.

In building from one lesson to plan the next, we center our work on four essential questions, the same four introduced in the beginning of this book:

1. What are our goals for student learning?

2. What can students now understand and do in relation to those goals?

3. What learning opportunities do we need to provide to help students build from current abilities to realize the goals?

4. What do we need to learn or change about our practice to provide those opportunities?

The OI debrief protocol helps us detail answers to Question 2, specific to the lesson goals. We describe evidence of what students do and say. We make generalizations. In the next step, we explore Questions 3 and 4 in more detail. We articulate cause-and-effect links between instructional opportunities and student learning. We identify approaches to replicate and approaches to change. Building from this information, we set goals for ourselves and our team and plan the next lesson.

Often the experience of planning, observing, and then debriefing a lesson in this sequence leads a team to make data-driven decisions as they plan the next lesson. They determine whether to refine, redesign, raise rigor, and/or release responsibility based on very specific observational data about students and shared goals.

How Do We Facilitate Deep Work?

The protocol itself is a powerful guide for courageous inquiry, but what can a facilitator do when there are challenges? What if a team glosses over what isn't working out of fear of conflict or struggle and misses a valuable learning opportunity? What if they conclude from observation data that the students have deficits, not that teaching needs to change?

How we respond to data is a pivotal moment in inquiry. How does data in one lesson drive how we plan the next? How do we respond when students don't succeed in a lesson? How do we respond when they do? In building from data to drive teaching, we stand at the crossroads of multiple opportunities—including options that will deepen our learning and options that will end it.

Let's explore possible pivot points in a team conversation and strategies a facilitator can use to drive deeper collaborative work. We'll explore these in two sections: learning from failure and responding to success.

Learning From Failure

Failure is an F word in many schools, a scarlet letter F to avoid at all costs. It's an experience most of us fear as educators and as administrators. Failure is not a word we use in discussing data or lessons with teams because it is a judgment word loaded with a history of baggage. Instead of saying a lesson fails, we get very specific about the challenges we noticed. Instead of saying we failed, we focus on opportunities. This growth-oriented language helps, and yet we must also be prepared to address the universal fear of failure head on. It is the elephant in the room anytime something isn't working. It's an elephant that can steer a team off course.

When we look at evidence that students are struggling, do we do the following:

- Take ownership or blame others?
- Personalize or stereotype?
- Embrace or avoid challenge?

How we respond to failure makes our breaks our impact as educators for equity. Let's explore the central issues of each of these pivotal choices with facilitator tips and questions that can help teams be courageous and committed in the face of challenges.

Take ownership or blame others? When we take ownership, we use evidence of student struggle as feedback about our instructional practice. We ask what we can change to get a different result. The opposite of ownership is blame. Students struggle because their parents didn't . . . , or previous teachers didn't . . . , or because poverty or other factors beyond a school's control are to blame.

Facilitator Tips and Questions to Foster Ownership

- Acknowledge that many factors beyond a school's control impact student achievement and that we will have the greatest impact on overcoming those challenges when we focus on what we can control:

instruction. Ask, "What can we as educators do within our class-rooms to help students?"

- Create together a graphic organizer of all the factors with the control of the school (within the circle) and beyond a schools' control (beyond the circle). Agree on a timesaving norm to "focus within our locus of control" and reference the chart whenever needed to bring the conversation back to specific steps for advancing educator impact.

Personalize or stereotype? When students struggle in a lesson, we can either get very specific about what these struggles tell us about their current levels of thinking, understanding, and learning needs, or we can draw general conclusions about what a group of kids can or can't do. Concluding from student struggle, a stereotype, such as, "Poor students can't . . . ," "ELLs can't . . . ," or "These kids don't know how to . . . ," fosters a fixed mindset—the belief that intelligence and talent are commodities that can't be changed. The implications for equity are profound as such statements steer teachers away from the ownership essential for reflection and instructional improvement and foster low expectations for students who most need the opportunity to excel.

The counterbalance to stereotyping is personalizing. We ask of our data questions to understand student thinking, motivation, prior knowledge, learning approach, and more. Rather than falling back on assumptions, we use data to get specific about our students as individuals on a continuum of learning. Sonia Claus Gleason and Nancy Gerzon advocate personalization as essential for equity, "A commitment to equity and excellence means recognizing that every child is a complex and compelling story, as a person and a learner" (2013, p. 4).

Facilitator Tips and Questions to Foster Personalization

- What do our data (from observations and assessments) tell us about the strengths and needs of individual students in our classrooms relative to our POP? What specifically can they now understand and do? What specific challenges do they demonstrate?
- What are the diverse ways students are responding to or engaging in the lesson? Describe differences in levels of understanding, participation, or performance and how to address them together.
- Does our current approach work for all students or just some students? If some still struggle, what can we do differently to meet their needs?

Embrace or avoid challenge? Many factors make it easy to avoid a challenge including fear of failure, fear of change, or fear of conflict.

After watching a lesson a colleague has taught and seeing that some aspects of the lesson led to student confusions, we may prefer to focus our conversation on the easy data of what worked. Celebration is valuable, but it can't be the only focus if we are to learn.

A growth mindset, the belief that intelligence and talent grow with effort is essential for collaborating to advance student learning and teacher learning. A key feature of a growth mindset, and an essential element of effective team inquiry, is a focus on challenges as opportunities.

Facilitator Tips and Questions to Foster a Growth Mindset to Embrace Challenges

- Foster imperfection in lesson planning. Encourage the team to plan in at least one opportunity that stretches their comfort zone and the comfort zone of kids. It will likely generate valuable data for the team.
- Model focusing on challenges. When you observe, gather evidence of student confusions or challenges, and share these indications of struggle among the data you prioritize. If you only focus on what is working for kids, others will think that is what they are supposed to do.
- Value challenges as opportunities. Emphasize that we learn the most from moments in teaching when students are confused, don't participate, or don't perform at the level of our expectations. Ask, "Were there any of these moments in this lesson? What can we learn from these moments about our students or about how we can shape teaching to meet their needs?"

Building From Successes

When students succeed with all of our expectations for a lesson, we reach a crossroads as well. Do we continue to teach in the same way to realize the same success? Do we raise rigor or release responsibility to move student learning along a progression toward a higher goal? Do we keep refining the same approach, or do we plan the next lesson with increased levels of complexity?

Refining a lesson multiple times across a year has many advantages for a team. Anytime students succeed in a lesson, this is usually the preferred path to take. It is valuable to refine a routine together and deepen expertise across different lesson contexts. It's also comforting to keep doing what works, rather than designing and testing new ways to teach. It can also be problematic to keep refining one approach to one type of lesson task when it holds students at a certain level of learning.

To make these choices, teams both zoom in to focus on the outcomes of the lesson and zoom out to consider the larger practice *and* the big picture of the POP.

Teams make the best decisions about how to proceed from lesson to lesson when they understand both the specifics of data from a lesson and consider the big picture view of where students are in relation to the end goal. A facilitator can help a team zoom in and out the frame of reference to consider these two perspectives by asking questions about our goal, the students, and the gap between the two. The following questions help teams focus beyond a short-term success to the next level of opportunity for growth:

- **Goal:** What is the end goal? When we solve our POP, what will success look like? What is the end task through which we measure success? How do those tasks compare to tasks in this lesson?
- **Students:** What did students demonstrate they can now understand and do relevant to our goal? Is success with this lesson the same as success with our POP?
- **Instruction:** What are the next instructional steps for students who have not yet reached the end goal? If students have not reached the end goal, what next instructional opportunities do they need to succeed? If they have, how will we extend and deepen learning?

In teaching for equity, where students often need to make more than one year of progress to access future opportunities, we especially must always hold in our minds two realities: where students are and where they need to be. We must continuously compare the formative data from right now to our future goal, and adjust instruction to ensure progress along a continuum of learning.

Reframing Is Essential for Raising Expectations

When the focus is on one lesson only, as with a demonstration lesson or isolated coaching session or single lesson study, sometimes teachers take the learning from that lesson as a rule to apply to all future lessons. For example, when one fourth-grade teacher observed his colleague have success structuring a classroom conversation using response frames, he then equated response frames with successful classroom conversations and used them for every conversation for the rest of the year.

In a lesson his team observed, students were demonstrating a readiness to engage in high-level discussion around a text. Their conversations froze and backtracked, however, as they followed the very structured response frames posted to guide the interaction.

This is a familiar scenario to many educators working in linguistically diverse schools. A scaffold that is effective in one scenario becomes "the rule," rather than a temporary help to release when students thrive. This happens all too often in the ELL arena, where scaffolds such as response frames become an expectation in lesson plans and administrator walk-throughs. Facilitators can challenge this practice by encouraging a shift in focus from the means (a strategy) to the end goal (student learning). Rather than asking, "Are teachers using response frames," ask, "Are students engaged in collaborative conversations about content? Are students using academic language in their discussions? How do scaffolds in the room impact student learning and participation?"

One of the most devastating moves we can make is to fixate on a specific scaffold as being an essential part of every lesson. It can be humbling to see a scaffold we love and have trained colleagues to use get in the way in a specific lesson. If you have such a moment, as I have, in which you see a strategy you recommended get in the way, take notes on specific evidence that leads you to that conclusion. Share that evidence both to encourage nuanced thinking about when and how to use scaffolds and to model the humility of learning from data. If we fixate on what we have always done, even when data prove us wrong, teachers will do the same. When we are flexible to learn and change, we inspire a team of learners.

REFLECTION QUESTIONS

- Which team story of deepening learning do you most relate to? Why? What detail in that story do you want to remember as you begin OI?
- How will you help teams move beyond "playing it safe" with planning, toward courageous risk taking to push a new edge of learning for their students and themselves?
- What is your ideal vision for a how a team will respond when a lesson reveals many challenges? What actions will you take as a facilitator to realize this vision?

10 Evaluating and Expanding Our Impact

"For all students to learn, educators and professional learning must be held to high standards. This is particularly important for schools that have English Language Learners, or language minority students."

—Margarita Calderón (Learning Forward, 2011)

Observation inquiry (OI) ends where it began: with a focus on impact. We set out to solve a problem of practice (POP) and answer inquiry questions. Across multiple lessons we tested approaches and refined and redesigned instruction. Within each lesson we analyzed evidence of impact, and we used that data to drive our teaching and professional learning. At the conclusion of a multilesson cycle of continuous inquiry, we now step back to ask, "What is the impact of this professional learning design?"

- What have our students learned?
- What have teachers learned? What shifts have teachers made in daily instruction?
- What impact has this had on the collaborative learning culture of our school?

We ask these questions honestly, aware that sometimes the data will give us cause for celebration and sometimes it will probe us to refine or redesign our approach. Sometimes we find answers, and other times we benefit from the learning opportunity of more questions to pursue.

In this chapter, we'll focus on impact including a combination of strategies for evaluating impact and specific results from teams featured in this book. We'll then build from this reflective process to the larger question of expanding impact beyond the individual teams to build multiteam synergy and reach more classrooms and schools.

We'll explore these topics in five sections, each to pursue a question:

- What have students learned?
- What have teachers learned?
- What has shifted in our adult learning culture?
- How do we share learning beyond the team?
- How do we expand impact in coming years?

"Professional learning that increases educator effectiveness and results for all students uses a variety of sources and types of student, educator, and system data to plan, assess, and evaluate professional learning."

—Learning Forward Data
Standard for Professional Learning

WHAT HAVE STUDENTS LEARNED?

The ultimate goal of all professional learning is to improve student learning. When it is effective, it is like a well-aligned domino in a sequence of cause and effect: professional learning impacts teacher learning impacts instruction impacts student learning. Line up a series of dominos strategically and you may find that sometimes that careful lineup we create to reach the end doesn't make it. A few dominos turned off course will halt the continuous momentum, and the last dominos stand unchanged. Such is the case with professional learning workshops that impact teacher *understanding*, but don't shift *instruction* in ways that ensure students learn.

In reflecting on impact, we begin with a focus on the ultimate goal: student learning. Within a team, we evaluate this in every lesson. Now at the end of a multilesson cycle, we take time to reflect back on how far students have come since the beginning of our work together. We use multiple measures, as possible, to help us measure student growth specific to our POP. These include the following:

Pre- and Postassessment Data

In Chapter 5, we focused on designing an assessment task aligned to our end goal, a valuable action to take at the beginning of inquiry to get specific about the goal and plan toward that end. When possible, teams create two versions of the assessment task and give one to students at the start of inquiry to establish a baseline of what students can do and to gather formative data to drive planning. At the end of a multilesson cycle of inquiry, teams use a similar task to assess student learning then compare the two to measure growth. The type of data a team gathers depends on their POP. Here are some examples of options:

Written responses. One fifth-grade team focused on engaging ELLs with writing inferential responses to texts and created an assessment aligned to a text in their curriculum. The assessment was simply three constructed response questions that students answered in writing. Teachers agreed on the scaffolds of the task for consistency and used a rubric to score answers. Their postassessment was with a different text at the end of the year using similar types of questions. Teachers used the same rubric to compare growth.

Collaborative conversations. At Kawana Academy of the Arts and Sciences, all teams focused on a schoolwide POP specific to advancing academic conversations about texts. Conversations are a dynamic outcome for pre- and postassessment measures, and the school found a solution by creating and using a shared rubric aligned to CCSS and California English Language Development (CA ELD) standards to evaluate how students interacted. In the fall, teams practiced evaluating filmed conversations to calibrate their scoring and build shared agreements about the goal. Comparative scores after four months of team inquiry revealed a significant elevation in collaborative conversations across the school.

Local assessments. Local assessment measures relevant to the POP are especially helpful for gathering pre- and postdata because they align directly to systems across the school. Local assessments may include literacy assessments, curriculum-embedded assessments in any content area, or tasks a team creates together to gather formative data. A first-grade team focused on the challenge of ELL students retelling stories used the retelling task in the Developmental Reading Assessment (DRA), a literacy assessment used by all teachers at their site, to measure pre- and postachievement and evaluate growth.

High-stakes tests. High-stakes tests administered once per year are a more challenging measure to use to measure impact, as teachers don't always have comparative data. Such is the case with the second-grade team that focused on multiple-meaning words based on very low scores in this area on the previous year's high-stakes test. After engaging in OI to address this challenge area, they realized significantly higher scores for their second graders on the high-stakes test. These data are promising, and they also have limitations for measuring growth as there are no predata for comparison for the same students, only the same grade level with different kids. To complement these data, the team created a short assessment task similar to the high-stakes test, which they used to gather pre- and postassessment data.

Notes From Observation Inquiry

In tandem with other measures of student learning, we gain valuable data about impact by revisiting notes from each lesson we observed together, especially each list of generalizations. Analyzing generalizations across the four lessons for trends is one way to gain insight into shifts with hard-to-quantify goals. Across the lessons, compare the generalizations of student actions, thinking, and participation. Here are some questions to guide this reflection:

- What patterns do you notice?
- What is the evidence of student growth or shifts in dynamics of classroom participation?
- What challenges remain?
- Reflect also on the shifts in the lesson tasks themselves: Did we increase rigor over time? Release responsibility? How did these shifts in tasks impact student learning?

Teacher Reflections

Teacher reflections on student learning are also important to bring into the conversation. In a team reflection meeting at the end of a year of inquiry, reflect on questions such as these:

- What gains have our students made this year relevant to our POP?
- What evidence is there of student growth?
- What challenges remain?

Student Reflections

Another source of qualitative data is student reflections. Some teams choose to interview students with questions about their experiences, learning, or shifts in instruction. Having students retell an experience in a classroom during a task relevant to the POP is often very formative, as it provides a team with descriptive data about the learning from students' point of view. A before and after interview helps a team identify shifts. Also, asking higher-level reflection questions about what students learned or how instruction impacted learning is a way for teams to gather feedback at the end of a lesson or cycle of inquiry.

WHAT HAVE TEACHERS LEARNED?

Moving one domino back in the lineup from student outcomes we ask, "How has this learning design impacted teachers' understandings and practice?" Multiple measures give us the best understanding, and also we must use the evaluation approach that works best for our time, resources, and purpose. When we look to examples in the research community, there is always a higher bar for how we measure impact, and it's a bar we cannot expect to hold ourselves to when we also work fulltime as leaders and teachers. That said, there are time-efficient ways to gather data that help us understand what teachers have learned and how they shifted their practice as a result of this work. Three data sources include

- Teacher self-reflections
- Administrator reflections of teacher learning
- Student reflections of shifts in instruction

To put each of these approaches to data collection in context, let's consider the goals. Outcome goals for professional learning will vary by context, as OI is a process that can be used to achieve many adult learning goals. Within the context of teaching for equity and ensuring the success of AELs, ELLs, students of color, and students in poverty, some goals are universal. No matter a district's umbrella goal, or the specific POP of a team, we aim to realize the following outcomes:

These are only a sample of possible outcome goals, and ones that OI in particular helps teachers realize. Through teachers reflections, administrator reflections, observational data, and student reflections, we continue to see elevation of understanding, beliefs, and practices in these areas.

As we consider different data sources, reflecting back on the KASAB framework (Figure 10.1) (Killion, 2008) of types of learning helps put feedback in perspective. Shifts in understanding, for example, are not the same as shifts in practice. Understanding, attitudes, skills and aspirations are all important, and we still need to get a clear picture of how learning in any of these areas impacts behaviors and practices.

Figure 10.1 Sample of Teacher Outcomes Goals

Type of Learning "KASAB" (Killion, 2008)	Teacher Outcome
Knowledge Teachers understand . . .	Specific to the POP, teachers understand: • What success looks like • Student strengths and prior knowledge • Student learning challenges and instructional needs • How to build language and thinking in tandem with content
Attitude Teachers believe . . .	Teachers believe . . . • All learners, especially ELLs, students of color, and students in poverty, are capable of excelling with rigorous academic expectations • Teacher actions impact student achievement • Risk-taking and mistakes are essential for learning
Skills/Capacities Teachers are able to . . . **Aspirations/Motivations** Teachers are motivated/driven to. . . **Behaviors/Practices** In ongoing instruction, teachers now . . .	Teachers . . . • Structure lesson tasks to ensure accountable participation and engagement of all students • Gather formative data in every lesson • Use formative data to drive instruction • Use scaffolds strategically to foster student independence with rigorous tasks • Structure academic conversations that engage all learners in advancing content and language learning • Collaborate in continuous, data-driven problem solving with colleagues

A good metaphor for me about the significant leap it often takes to move from the first four KASABs to behavior change is my experience with exercise, specifically yoga. I like to do yoga as an exercise and for relaxation. I understand the value of this practice. I believe it is good for my health. I have the skills to do yoga poses on my own, and even the props I need. I'm motivated to do so. When it comes to behaviors, I must admit, I only practice yoga a few times a month.

For all of my understanding, attitude, skills, and motivation central to yoga to actually impact my health, I have yet to change my behavior. The same is true for teaching. For teacher understandings, attitudes, skills, and motivation to impact student learning, there must be a shift in instruction. These are the shifts we must measure to evaluate the impact of professional learning. How do we measure shifts in instruction? Let's begin with teacher reflections.

Teacher Reflections

Within a team, we gather personal and relevant details about impact by reflecting on our learning and changes we have made in teaching or seen in student learning as a result of this work. Qualitative data gathered through interviews, team reflections, or written surveys are valuable feedback for leaders looking to understand the impact of a professional learning model. Personal reflections, while difficult to quantify, illuminate evidence learning more specific and nuanced than a survey or numerical analysis can reveal.

As a facilitator, I always conclude a year of inquiry by always asking a team to reflect on five questions:

1. As a result of participating in this process, what shifts, if any, have you made in your teaching practice?

2. What shifts, if any, have you noticed with your students?

3. Which aspects of OI were most beneficial for your learning?

4. Which were least effective?

5. What would you change about the process?

The first question helps us understand teacher perceptions of their learning. The second question, focused on student learning, adds a qualitative element to the student data we gathered through multiple measures. The last questions are for direct feedback on the model to help us understand through teachers' eyes what is working in the structure of our learning design, how it is working, and what to refine or change.

Elevated Expectations and Ownership. Listening to teachers' personal answers to the first question has changed my life. Across diverse grade levels, subject areas, and districts with dramatically different cultures of collaboration, I've seen consistent themes in teacher reflections including first and foremost a shift from a focus on delivery to a focus on student learning. This is substantial in the arena of teaching for equity as a focus on student learning includes a sense of teacher ownership and efficacy for the learning of ELLs, students of color, and students in poverty. Instead of saying, "I taught but they didn't learn," we say, "They didn't learn, and now I'm adjusting how I teach." There is a shift from saying, "They can't do it" to, "I can ensure they do." The following quotes are a small sample of the types of reflections teachers share:

> "In forcing myself to look at the students and not the teacher, I'm getting more out of watching think-pair-share in my own classroom. I'm focusing more on the students than the teacher. I was thinking about me, my delivery. My instruction is important, yes, but I won't know

how good it is until I listen to their talk. It was an epiphany for me."
Heidi O'Hare, Mark West Elementary School

Erin Earnshaw, a middle school teacher of many AELs including ELLs and students poverty reflected, "I think we often get stuck thinking what kids can't do and how we are limited by what they can and can't do. (Observation inquiry) helps to shift the focus to us as teachers and how we can take them and what are the things we can do to get them farther."

A fifth-grade teacher on a multigrade team reflected after a second-grade lesson, "After having seen this lesson, I can say this (task in which ELLs compare themes across texts) really does seem doable. But this morning, I thought it wasn't . . . I didn't know you could get that much out of them. They are quite capable!"

Hearing teachers across multiple districts reflect on elevated expectations and ownership for the achievement of diverse learners was data that challenged me to stop and reflect on my career path as a consultant. As leader of workshops on effective strategies for ELLs, I, too, had been focusing on delivery. When I began leading deep work with teams, and listening to the impact, I evolved as a learning leader. I realized that talking about high expectations would likely change little, whereas rolling up our sleeves at the ground level to realize high expectations was essential for realizing equity in linguistically and culturally diverse schools.

Deeper Understandings of Students. Other shifts teachers reflect on include a deeper understanding of students, such as veteran teacher Pam Kelly's insight that she learned more about her students in one year than she ever had in the past. By focusing on the students who weren't participating and identifying their needs, she learned specifics about individuals including that one boy was terrified of making mistakes and one girl was scared of boys. This personalized knowledge of students helped her teach in ways that would reach every child.

Shifts in Teaching and Student Learning. The following video is an example of an informal conversation among teachers to reflect on their participation in OI. This is a first-grade team at a Title I school with a high population of ELLs. The POP they worked to address was, "When discussing stories using reading strategies, students are challenged to respond orally in complete sentences." The team worked specifically on fostering partner conversations about text in which all students engaged in extended discussions together. Listen as they reflect on student learning and their own learning for evidence of shifts in teacher knowledge, attitude, skills, aspirations, or behaviors/teaching practice.

Scan the following QR code to access the video:

Reflect on the Video

- What shifts did students notice in student learning and participation?
- What shifts did teachers identify in their practice?
- What are benefits and limitations of using informal reflections to evaluate impact?

A Mindset for Collaborative Risk Taking. In the following video, a middle school teacher reflects on what she most valued in the OI process. As you watch consider her mindset about collaboration and risk taking.

Scan the QR code to access the videos:

Reflect on the Video

- What does this quote reveal about her attitude and beliefs about teacher collaboration and risk taking?
- Did her experience collaborating in OI have a role in shaping this mindset? How can we know?

Quantifying Reflections With a Survey. A survey is another approach for gathering qualitative data. Open-ended questions are similar to an interview, but with a sense of privacy, especially if the survey is anonymous. Questions with a scaled response can also help quantify results on impact. In addition to guiding reflection within teams, I also use a survey in which teachers evaluate statements using a scale, such as strongly disagree, disagree, somewhat agree, agree, and strongly agree.

A survey including a scaled response is especially helpful for synthesizing reflection data across multiple schools or districts. For example, after leading teams in OI in three districts, I surveyed participants about shifts they made in instruction and shifts they observed in student learning specific to our goals.

Across diverse districts and grade levels, in every team surveyed, teachers reflected that they increased their emphasis on engaging *all* students in key lesson conversations and tasks. The following percentages in parentheses show how many teachers agreed or strongly agreed that as a result of their participating in this process, they now

- Structure more peer-to-peer conversations as part of daily instruction (100%)
- Structure more accountable tasks to check for understanding (100%)
- Have higher expectations for students' oral language use (94%)
- Deepened expertise in addressing their teams' POP (96%)

Even though data in a survey are quantifiable and can be charted in official graphs, remember that numbers do not represent the absence of bias. These results indicate teachers' perceptions of change, a powerful measure and an exciting indicator to celebrate in combination with other types of data that help us understand the impact of our professional learning design.

Limitations of Reflections. Personal reflections are valuable data, and also have the limitation of being filtered through the lens of an individual's biases and self-perceptions. Reflections in a group setting might also be influenced by the dynamics of the group and culture of safety. Reflections in a personal interview will vary depending on the relationship between the people in the conversation. Reflections elicited in a survey will vary depending on whether the survey is anonymous, who will read the survey, and the levels of trust involved. Even with the highest levels of trust and best culture for shared risk taking, individuals will vary how they present themselves based on perceptions and personality.

Reflections are still a rich source of data on the impact of OI, specifically with regard to teacher perceptions about changes in student learning and changes in instructional practice and mindsets for collaboration with colleagues. We enhance our understanding of impact by also seeking other types of evidence.

Administrators Reflections and Observation Data

Administrator reflections are also subjective and have limitations as a data source, but they add to our big picture understanding of impact. Beyond self-reflection within a team, engage the site administrator(s) in reflecting on the impact of this work. What shifts, if any, have there been in the school as a result of this work? Describe the shifts and how you know. Consider, for example, shifts in the following:

- How teachers teach
- How teachers collaborate
- How teachers discuss linguistically and culturally diverse students
- Student participation

Maureen Rudder, principal at McDowell Elementary School reflected only a few months after teams engaged in OI, "There is already a shift in how teachers are using their planning time together. There is less of a focus on just planning, and more on reflecting on student learning and refining instruction to meet their needs."

What sources of data do administrators use to draw conclusions about shifts in teaching and professional collaboration? Consider

- Walk-through observations
- Formal observations
- Instructional rounds or other collaborative approaches to school-wide observation
- Listening to how teachers collaborate

The essential question for any of these data to be formative is, What are administrators listening for and looking for? When team learning goals align with local initiatives, as is recommended in Chapter 4, there is a natural connection between the challenges teams are solving and the challenges the school as a whole focuses on together. With alignment, there is a natural connection between what administrators look for and listen for in classrooms and what teachers are trying to change. Goals are clear, and all work in synthesis to identify what is needed to achieve them.

In schools focused on elevated academic conversations for ELLs, a major focus of many teams in this book, principals walk into classrooms looking to see who is doing the talking and what ELL students in particular are doing during key lesson tasks. In these contexts, administrators reflect on shifts in classroom discourse from hand-raising to partner and group discussions, from ELL passivity to active participation of all students.

Integrating Data From Instructional Rounds

Other ways to gain a big picture perspective on shifts in instruction include using a collaborative observation process such as instructional rounds, a practice in which administrators and teachers observe multiple classrooms in a school to gather evidence specific to a POP (City, Elmore,

Fiarman, & Teitel, 2009). Kawana Academy of Arts and Sciences, a Title I charter elementary school, had been using the instructional rounds process before starting OI. They then used both processes in the following year: one for schoolwide inquiry and one for teams. After a year of OI, they noticed significant difference in the data collected during schoolwide rounds. Observers, a combination of teachers and administrators, noticed that in every classroom across the school all learners were discussing lesson content with peers. Teachers were structuring partner and small group interactions, a shift from the previous year when many tasks involved hand raising, where many students, especially ELLs, were silent. When there is pre- and postdata especially, data from instructional rounds are another potential source of information for evaluating the impact of professional learning across a school.

Using Multiple Measures

While no individual way of measuring impact is perfect, the use of multiple measures in tandem helps us understand trends. When evaluating the impact of OI from a leadership perspective, use a combination of student learning data, teacher reflections, administrator reflections, and other relevant sources to help reflect on impact. The questions we ask as professional learning leaders are similar to the questions we ask ourselves as teachers and as teams:

- What impact has this professional learning design had on student and teacher learning?
- In what specific ways did we realize our goals for students and teachers?
- What can we learn from our successes?
- What can we learn from our challenges?
- What are our next steps for advancing student and teacher learning?

Our reflections and analysis of impact help guide our work and also illuminate opportunities to share learning and discoveries across teams.

HOW DO WE EXPAND LEARNING BEYOND THE TEAM?

Growing as individual teams and realizing gains for our students is a valuable end in itself, and there is potential to leverage this work as a catalyst for cross-team synergy. Does the learning end with our team, or do we share our findings with others? Do our new questions for inquiry end with our team, or do we engage colleagues across a site, district, or online community to seek and discover new solutions together?

Benefits of reaching beyond our team or facilitating collaboration across teams include the potential to

- impact more teachers and students;
- inspire others to engage in collaborative inquiry; and
- build a network of educators focused on shared challenges and questions that matter.

What do we share? How do we share it? How do we move from simply reporting to igniting cross-team synergy and new networks of collaboration?

What Do We Share?

While there are many ways to share what we have learned, including writing articles or books for publication, few educators have the time or interest in developing a detailed report. Professional learning is practical, and the best action to take with it is in the classroom to improve learning for kids. The key to facilitating sharing is making it time-efficient for teachers.

One strategy is to make the format simple and connected to the reflection teams already engage in at the end of their work. Figure 10.2 Team Reflection on Impact offers one option for a clear and concise format to gather key findings for reflection and sharing beyond the team.

Why Hypothesize?

Across multiple lessons, teams use a myriad of strategies to adjust and modify instruction to get results. In reflecting on their process overall, a team hypothesizes which actions lead to the gains in student learning to keep those at the forefront of their teaching practice and shared those specific strategies with others.

The word "hypothesize" is intentional in this question to remove the pressure of absolute certainty and to invite possibilities to further test and refine findings. Hypothesis is a more accurate term as, by design, OI is helping teachers effectively advance and integrate approaches to realize gains for students. In this dynamic process, teams don't control for all variables and scientifically test one approach. We don't, for example, randomly assign students and teachers to different classrooms and then change only one variable in half the classrooms so that we can compare the results. Leave that controlled type of study to the research arena, as the work of enhancing teaching involves multiple variables shifting in tandem to meet student needs. Given this complexity, it is tough to draw absolute conclusions and teams may be hesitant to share what they learned.

Figure 10.2 Team Reflection on Impact

School(s):_____ Year: _____

Subject Area(s): _____ Grades: _____

1. **Problem of Practice:**

2. **Beginning of the Year Student Challenges: (Summarize evidence)**

3. **End of Year Student Successes: (Summarize evidence)**

4. **Instructional Actions We Hypothesize Led to These Student Successes:**

5. **Questions/Challenges for Future Inquiry:**

Figure 10.3 Second-Grade Example: Team Reflection on Impact

1. **Problem of Practice:** Based on state and local testing data we choose, students, especially ELLs, are not making sense of multiple-meaning words within the context of their reading.

2. **Beginning of the Year Student Challenges:**

   • Most students could not perform the state assessment task of matching a sentence to a sentence that uses the same meaning of the word, even with text read aloud.

   • When given a matching and sorting tasks, most pairs could not complete the task with discussion. Often one partner just grabbed the papers and did the work silently.

   • Most students could not justify why they matched the sentence to the meaning.

3. **End of Year Student Successes:**

   • Students are more word conscious in all homerooms. They are word detectives, finding multiple meaning words in many contexts outside of vocabulary lessons.

   • All performed the final state assessment tasks without hesitation.

   • Majority performed three out of four tasks correctly after reading the sentences independently.

   • ELLs in all classrooms continue to work collaboratively in pair task, and take roles in an ongoing dialogue. They ask the question, share a response, justify, agree, and/or disagree.

4. **Instructional Actions We Hypothesize Led to These Student Successes:**

   • Using a consistent visual (circle map) and instructional routine across multiple lessons.

   • Gradual release of responsibility toward independent success with the ultimate task: We started with initial skills and multiple scaffolds, then pulled back on scaffolds and intensified the demands. For example, initially students matched sentence to meaning by pointing to meaning on the circle map, then sorted color-coded meanings on the map. In a subsequent lesson, we removed the color-coding, then removed the map. Finally, students completed a multiple-choice task similar to the state task, and then justified their response to a partner.

   • Writing, modeling, and practicing a dialogue (ask, state and justify, agree/disagree) to help all partners participate in a multiple-step conversation to help one another with the thinking and language demands of the task.

5. **Questions/Challenges for Future Inquiry:**

   • How do students go beyond disagreement? Some already know and are extending conversations in partnerships. Others stop the conversation immediately when there is a disagreement. How can we help students continue to explore ideas together when they disagree so that they can learn from one another's different perspective?

Embrace this hesitancy as the healthy uncertainty of critical thinkers, and also ask that it not stand in the way of sharing their findings. It's valuable that teams ask of every conclusion, "How do we know this strategy leads to the student outcome I want?" It's valuable that teachers ask this every day by watching students for evidence of what works and does not work.

For this reason, we draw conclusions together as "hypotheses of actions that lead to student success." This phrasing invites teachers to bring the strategies that appear to be most effective to the forefront, and encourages all to continue testing them with an eye toward the ultimate litmus test of any educational solution: student learning.

Teams share conclusions with an invitation for more questions, more inquiry, and further opportunities to push the edge of both teacher and student learning.

Sharing Learning

Our approach to sharing findings may be as simple as a report of learning or as dynamic as a multiteam conference building synergy across schools. Let's explore some of the options.

Report as FYI

Quick ways for a team to share learning include distributing the Team Reflection on Impact page in a site or district newsletter, sharing it at a meeting, or posting it in an online blog with invitation for comments and insights from an expanded professional learning network. The benefits of these forms of sharing are convenience. Teams use an existing meeting structure or publication channel to distribute their findings and reflection.

Report as Catalyst

The drawback of an FYI approach is the communication is typically one-way. When others read or hear a team's report they get an update. They may take away a key strategy or idea to apply to teaching practice, or not. Enhance any FYI approach by using the report as a catalyst to facilitate an exchange of ideas. For example, ask others to reflect on their experience with the team's POP and tested solutions. Invite discussion, debate, and new perspectives. Another excellent opportunity for rich discourse is the topic of unresolved challenges and questions for future inquiry. Any learning team, no matter how many successes they realize, typically identifies at least one new question for inquiry or unresolved challenge to solve. It's the nature of teaching for equity: Our problems are complex, and there is always an opportunity to learn and grow. Specify the challenges or questions and ask, "How can we collaborate to learn more about these questions and to solve these challenges across all classrooms?"

Building Multiteam Synergy

When many teams across a site or district engage in continuous team inquiry, consider leading a miniconference to facilitate cross-team synergy.

Petaluma City Schools used this approach to bring two Title I schools together to reflect on learning, share findings, and collaborate to address new challenges. All grade-level teams across the kindergarten through third-grade school and the fourth- through sixth-grade school engaged in inquiry to advance language and literacy for ELLs. Within the context of this umbrella goal, each team worked on a POP across the year. As a facilitator of each team, I often noticed that insights from one team could help another team and wanted to find a way to support a more expansive exchange of ideas. In addition, there was a trend in the "aha" insights about challenges and unanswered questions: many teachers were focusing on the same new issues and challenges we could only address by collaborating dynamically across the K–6 continuum.

We structured the three-hour afternoon conference with the three key activities:

- Team sharing to learn from one another
- Cross-team dialogue to problem solve together
- Team planning to identify priorities for inquiry in the coming year

Team sharing. Teams had a maximum of 10 minutes to present, and used the Figure 10.2 Team Reflection on Impact page to share the essentials. There was no pressure to create elaborate presentations, so busy teachers could feel comfortable sharing ideas without the stress of trying to create a "show" for colleagues in the final busy weeks of the school year. The reflection page reduced preparation time by narrowing the task to five essentials that can be listed with bullet points, and the common format also made it easy for readers to take in information from multiple teams. Teams with specific visuals from a lesson or strategy (e.g., circle map to teach multiple-meaning words) shared those as well.

Cross-team dialogue. At three points between the presentations, we structured a cross-team dialogue about an unanswered question or challenge universal to kindergarten through sixth grade. Planning this feature involved three elements:

- Identifying unanswered questions and challenges that would be a priority to discuss
- Structuring seating so each table involved people from multiple teams
- Scheduling key discussion points between the team presentations

Prioritizing questions. Use Figure 10.2 Team Reflection on Impact to gather questions from teams, as the last task is questions/challenges for further inquiry. Read the questions/challenges each team wrote in their reflection, or if you facilitated the teams, reflect on the challenges teams identified together. Choose one to three questions/challenges that are universal for teams that will participate in the multiteam discussion.

The questions we chose in Petaluma follow. As you read these questions, note that the solution to each lives beyond any individual grade level or content area. Cross-team collaboration and synergy is critical to address these coherently across a multigrade continuum. The teachers discussed the following questions at three collaboration points in the conference:

- How do we build success of reluctant participants?
- How can we help students move from passivity to initiative and risk taking?
- How do we equip students with tools to expand and justify thinking across the grades?
- How do we build from framed and scripted responses to dynamic student conversations about content learning?

Synthesizing Elements Into an Agenda

Notice in the example agenda, Figure 10.4, each of three discussion questions follows a short set of team presentations. We clustered presentations according to similarities in their problems of practice and/or similarities in the new challenges and questions they uncovered through their work. This gave the discussion a dual purpose: time to process what teams had shared *and* time to collectively brainstorm ways to address a key challenge or question the teams identified that is relevant to all classrooms.

Planning Questions

In planning a miniconference, consider these questions:

- **Outcomes:** What are your primary goals for this miniconference? To share ideas? To fuel new questions? To build cross-team synergy? To

Figure 10.4 Example Miniconference Agenda

Advancing K–6 Learning

McDowell and McKinley Team Miniconference

McDowell School Library, May 16th, 2012

Facilitator: Tonya Ward Singer

1:15 Welcome and Introduction

1:22 Getting Students Talking: Kindergarten

Building Dialogue: 1st Grade

Pair-Share Brainstorm: How do we build K–6 success of reluctant participants?

Analyzing Language Needs: 3rd Grade

Inferring and Justifying: 4th Grade

2:07 *Discussion: How can we help students move from passivity to initiative and risk taking across the K–6 continuum?*

2:27 Multiple-Meaning Words and Justifying Responses: 2nd Grade

Rigor, Relevance, and Inferential Thinking: 5th Grade

Using Context Clues to Infer Meaning: 6th Grade

2:57 *Discussion: How do we equip students with the tools to expand and justify responses across the grades? How do we build from framed and scripted responses, to dynamic, student conversations about content learning?*

3:35 Focus Priorities for 2012/2013. Reseat by Grade Level. Brainstorm and list possible POP focus ideas for 2012/2013.

3:50 Conclusion and Next Steps

4:00 *End*

articulate programs? To inspire more teachers to open their doors to deep, collaborative inquiry? Make sure your answer to these questions drives how you answer all that follow.

- **Time:** When is the most convenient time to bring people together? How much time will you need? How will you structure the time available to achieve your top priority outcomes?
- **Participation:** Who will participate? Will you involve multiple schools, grade-levels, or departments? Will you involve only teams who share their learning or also others new to this work?
- **Content:** What is the priority content for teams to share? What new questions are priorities to discuss?
- **Format:** How will teams share ideas? Consider presentations, poster-sessions, interactive social-media, or other formats.
- **Interaction:** How will you structure interactive activities to engage teachers in exploring ideas across teams?
- **Flow:** How will you integrate these elements into a cohesive agenda that has a sense of flow for every participant? How will you balance sitting with movement and listening with collaborative reflection and action?

HOW DO WE SUSTAIN CONTINUOUS LEARNING?

> *"Change is the only constant in life."*
>
> —Heraclitus

After leading teams into classrooms together to engage in a yearlong cycle of inquiry, what happens next? How do build on successes to scale up our impact? How do we learn from challenges to refine or redesign our approach?

The following four leadership strategies are effective ways to fuel the long-term success of OI for deep collaborative learning:

1. Build capacity for facilitation.

2. Put intention on the calendar.

3. Apply OI to new contexts.

4. Maintain the mindset.

Build Capacity for Facilitation

Build the capacity of educators within your school or district to be facilitators of OI. In addition to involving coaches and specialists as facilitators, invest in classroom teachers as leaders for OI. The impact of this has a ripple effect, both on the OI process and on the depth of other forms of collaboration within a school. Build facilitator capacity via the following actions:

- Provide facilitator workshops before each OI cycle.
- Support facilitators with coaching or cofacilitation.
- Build facilitator networks either locally or online to engage facilitators in collaborating to share strengths and address challenges together.
- Elicit ongoing feedback from facilitators about what is working, what is challenging, and what additional support they may need.
- Build shared leadership in every OI team by having the facilitator release responsibility to participants. After facilitating the protocol steps for the first few lessons, for example, have participants take turns facilitating transitions through the protocol. Use Appendix B as an easy reference guide for any participant to lead the protocol.
- At the conclusion of each OI cycle, recruit and retain facilitators for the coming year.

Put Intention on the Calendar

The simple act of scheduling makes or breaks a good plan. One school with a powerful momentum for OI in year one was slow to self-start in the following year. When I interviewed the teachers and administrators about their situation, I learned they looked forward to OI and were ready to invest in release days for the collaborative observation, but hadn't taken action because they didn't have dates on the calendar.

One simple and powerful action a leader can take is to help a team plan the logistics of who, what, where, and when in advance. Use the Team Contact and Scheduling Page, at the QR link below for easy, efficient planning. This works well as a short meeting for returning teams or part of a launch workshop for new teams (See Appendix A for details).

Use this QR code to access the Team Contact and Scheduling Page:

Apply OI to New Contexts

A powerful leadership strategy is to help others with flexible thinking. Sometimes when educators learn OI in one context such as the umbrella goal and team's POP, they associate the process only with that one context. This is problematic when the context changes and people miss the opportunity to apply the same OI *process* to solve other challenges in education. For example, if a district uses OI with a focus on mathematical problem solving, for example, many participants will associate OI with mathematical problem solving. The next time the district focus changes from mathematical problem solving toward a new goal such creativity and innovation in the classroom, educators assume that OI must also be dropped. The faulty assumption is that OI is about mathematical problem solving.

For long-term success with OI, help others separate *context* from *process*. Use OI as a *process* for collaborative learning with whatever goal is most important for your team, school, or district. Teams that separate *context* from *process* know that a change in goals is not a reason to end OI, but rather an invitation apply their expertise in collaborative OI to pursue new questions and solve new problems.

The diverse examples in this book are intentional to help readers see how OI can be used in different contexts. There are even more possibilities to explore. Share diverse examples with teams to help them realize that the process lives beyond the context of what we are solving right now, this year in this team. When goals shift, help educators leverage their expertise with the OI process to engage in deep inquiry about the challenges and questions specific to those new outcome goals.

Maintain the Mindset

Sustaining success is entirely about sustaining a mindset for continuous, collaborative inquiry to identify and address needs. It's not about making one learning design a permanent fixture in a new status quo. It's about asking continuously

- What are our goals for professional learning?
- What student outcomes do we want to realize as a result of professional learning?
- What shifts in teacher practice do we hope to see?
- What resources do we have to achieve those goals?
- How can we best leverage resources to "integrate theories, research, and models of human learning to achieve *our* intended outcomes?" (Learning Forward)

The word "integrate" in this standard implies flexibility. Districts that sustain dynamic professional learning sustain a focus on a problem or goal until they solve it, and are nimble in shifting and adjusting approaches to leverage resources and realize success.

Compare these different ways districts sustain a commitment to engaging teachers in continuous inquiry around live lessons year to year:

1. **Scale up OI.** Have participants become facilitators of new teams. Build capacity for sustainability with ongoing professional learning for facilitators. Follow-up with teams to monitor and support continued success.

2. **Take turns.** When resources limit how many teachers can participate, rotate which teams participate in OI each year. A turn-taking approach works best when existing teams (e.g., grade-level or subject area) engage in OI so that the shared understandings and expertise they develop in classrooms together enhances their long-term collective work.

3. **Adapt.** Vary the model as appropriate to best use your resources to realize your goals. A model that complements OI is peer pair inquiry (PPI), a protocol for engaging partners, rather than teams, in observing and debriefing lessons together. Scan this QR code to access a full description and reproducible template for leading PPI:

4. **Integrate.** In schools with a working PLC model, integrate the collaborative observation and analysis of lessons into the cycle of work teachers lead in collaborative team meetings. This cuts down on the release time teachers need as they complete all of the following during their PLC meeting time: analyze assessment results, identify challenges, identify solutions, plan an approach to test, and report back with findings.

As in teaching, the end goal is never the use of a strategy but student learning; professional learning, the end goal is never the use of an approach but the deepening of teacher learning. I encourage readers to reflect back on the two primary purposes of this book:

1. Equip readers with tools to implement OI

2. Fuel a mindset of continuous inquiry about impact that is essential for this, or any professional learning model to make a difference for *all* students.

The first offers a path, and the second challenges readers to question every path, even OI. The second goal ultimately is more important than the first. It must be, or OI becomes another silver-bullet solution, an end in itself.

When we use OI, not as an end goal but as a *process* for realizing the outcomes that most matter for our schools, our possibilities are limitless. When we dare to question our impact, no matter what the data reveal, and adjust our approach continuously until we get results, we will solve challenges of inequity in 21st-century schools.

Continuous, Courageous Learning

Whether we are administrators, professors, coaches, consultants, or teachers, we are *all* learners standing on the edge of possibility.

Do we leap? Or do we stand on the familiar ground of what we know, where unequal opportunities are the reality for kids living in poverty, students of color, and ELLs, where even successful students graduate underprepared for 21st-century careers?

Do we play it safe by teaching behind closed doors and only collaborating with colleagues around what we know and understand?

Or do we dare step together from the secure footing of what we know right now, today, to ask the next level of questions to which we don't have answers and embrace the challenges we have yet to solve?

Whether we create equal opportunities for kids comes down to our courage to change and lead change. The next generation depends on our commitment as educators to be nimble problem solvers who collaborate to create new possibilities.

What are your next steps, as a learner and a leader, when you reflect on the question that drove me to write this book and continues to shape my learning:

How can we best leverage our actions to reach every child?

The more I ask this question, the more I see the expansive possibilities for how we can answer it. This is not a multiple-choice question, or even an essay with a rubric response. Every answer leads to new questions. Questions ultimately are our greatest tools for learning.

What questions drive you?

What challenges do you aim solve?

How will you leverage your actions to reach every child?

APPENDIX A

Launching Observation Inquiry

Beginning observation inquiry (OI) with teachers new to the process is in many ways like launching a rocket. We work through logistics and planning, and then we orchestrate a synthesis of multiple factors to launch our collaboration into flight.

When teams are new to beginning OI, there is typically a similar pattern to getting started. Initially, there is fear or uncertainty about watching one another teach. A facilitator works the ground level, bringing everyone into the process. It is a gravity-rich environment where nothing will fly without help.

Initially, a leader launching OI works hard: building buy-in, guiding, coaching, and preparing the team. Once teams share a focus and plan and observe the first lesson together, a momentum builds. Teams move forward together, driven by their curiosity and delving into specifics that help them make a difference for kids. A leader's role is no longer to lead, but to initiate the momentum, to witness and facilitate a dynamic flight.

This appendix focuses on how to get started at ground level with a workshop to launch OI for teachers new to the process. Here I synthesize activities and concepts from the book into a cohesive workshop that builds the buy-in, trust, shared vision, and protocol skills needed to begin inquiry.

The Launch Workshop Overview

The OI launch is one of my favorite workshops to lead as it always involves a shift: from fear to trust, from uncertainty to clarity, from individuals to team. This is the day we set the tone, build the trust and protocols, and spark the questions and process that ignite a yearlong inquiry. How we begin and our sequence of activities matter both for the content we discuss and for addressing the important emotional factors essential for collective change.

Purpose: Initiate a cycle of inquiry that supports teacher teams in collaborating to plan, teach, and analyze student learning to advance student learning.

Outcomes: Participants will

- build trust and risk taking in collegial teams;
- learn and apply a nonevaluative approach to observing and debriefing lessons;
- identify a high-leverage student challenge area; and
- plan team inquiry for the year.

When? Most schools structure the launch workshop before the school year begins or within the first two months of school. Often the workshop is a release day, but it can also be a series of afterschool meetings.

Who? Participants are usually teams signed up to participate, but they can also include teachers across a school or district learning about OI before forming teams.

What and how? I'll first detail the activities of the agenda into sections according to purpose to help you build metaawareness about design so you can make strategic modifications as needed to align with goals in your unique context. After outlining the sequence I use in one day, I'll share variations in the flow that are powerful options for teams that have additional time to launch OI.

We will explore the agenda in three sections that work as a cohesive flow and can also be separate miniworkshops.

Workshop Agenda

As you read each section and activity throughout the agenda, think about the shared experiences and prior knowledge of participants in your context. For each activity, ask yourself these questions:
- What is the purpose of this activity?
- What prior knowledge or shared experience do participants already have with this?
- How can I best connect to and build on their prior knowledge?
- What modifications would I make in approach or timing of this agenda activity to build on prior knowledge and address the specific needs of participants in my context?

Launch Part 1: Build Buy-In and Trust

The purpose of the first part of the launch workshop is to build buy-in and trust and to introduce the OI process. These activities can be led at an entire school or district-level meeting in which teachers are learning about the process prior to choosing to be on teams. They can also be used with teams who have signed up for OI, to build the essential trust for deep work. For each activity, see the page references for where to access a complete activity description.

Agenda Activity	Minutes	Directions
Welcome mixer. Pair discuss one of the following questions: (1) "What inspires you to teach?" (2) "If you could wave a magic wand and equip your students with one skill or ability, what would it be?"	10	Ch. 3 p. 42
Inquiry cycle overview. Briefly introduce the process, and explain the cycle using the graphic from Chapter 2.	10	Ch. 2 p. 21
Building teamwork. Brainstorm hopes and fears Write norms	60	Ch. 3 pp. 45, 48

Reflect

- When and where will I lead this part of the launch workshop? Will I recruit teams first, or use this to introduce the process before recruiting teams?
- What modifications will I make in approach or timing of this agenda to build on prior knowledge and address the specific needs of participants in my context?

Launch Part 2: Practice Observing and Debriefing Lessons Together

The next goal in the launch workshop is to help participants learn and use the protocols for observing and debriefing lessons. We begin with a focus on describing without judgment, as this is key to building trust and buy-in, then move to learning and practicing the protocol steps.

Agenda Activity	Minutes	Directions
Describing without judgment • Play a game to distinguish descriptions from judgment. • Practice describing student actions in a short video clip.	15	Ch. 6 pp. 94–96 p. 95
Introduce and practice protocol with a video lesson • Learn the steps of the protocol with the overview in Appendix B. • Practice observing and debriefing a 5–10 minute video of a lesson.	70	Appendix B Ch. 7 pp. 124–125

Live lesson variation: The most powerful way to train teams in the protocol is to lead them through the observation and debrief process around a live lesson. It's tough to fit this into the tight agenda of a single-day launch workshop, but possible if you omit the video practice and keep the lesson short. That said, I prefer to plan this next learning step as the first follow-up to the team launch. That way the team can plan the lesson together during the launch workshop and be invested in what they observe. This shared experience moves the talk about opening doors from the abstract to the concrete, and it helps them apply their knowledge of the protocol to action. As Confucius pointed out years ago, experience is the best teacher: "I hear and I forget. I see and I remember. I do and I understand."

Reflect

- When and where will I lead this part of the launch workshop?
- What video(s) will I use to practice observing together? If from an online source, will I download them in advance to my computer, or access them online during the workshop via a reliable internet connection?
- What modifications will I make in approach or timing of this agenda to build on prior knowledge and address the specific needs of participants in my context?

LAUNCH PART 3: INITIATE TEAM INQUIRY

The third essential part of the launch training is to engage teams in beginning their inquiry process together. This is where we delve into the content of Chapters 4 and 5: writing a problem of practice (POP) and identifying questions that matter. We then plan formative task(s) and identify specifically what success will look like. Next we plan our first lesson to teach and observe together.

Agenda Activity	Minutes	Directions
Write a POP.	35–90	Ch. 4
Identify how students will demonstrate success.	30–90	Ch. 4
Schedule lessons for inquiry.	15	Below
Plan the first lesson.	60–90	Ch. 4

Scheduling Our Lessons for Inquiry

Take time during or before the launch training workshop to create a yearlong schedule for the work. It sounds too easy to be so important, as this is primarily a logistical task. But don't underestimate the power of putting intention on the calendar. Use the Team Contact and Scheduling Page to decide up front when to teach each lesson, who will teach each lesson, and when and where the team will meet.

Scan the following QR code for quick access to the Team Contact and Scheduling Page:

While completing the organizer, also have all participants put the dates on their calendars, and have administrators add these dates to the school or district calendar.

I recommend facilitating scheduling toward the end of a launch workshop, after participants have engaged in a series of activities designed to build their trust and engagement with the team learning process. Scheduling who will teach each lesson is a turning point for teams new to the process. It is when we move from theory to action: individuals make a date and time commitment to open their doors to collaborative observation. There can be some nervous laughing at this stage, and I consistently find that, by this point, people are ready to sign up to teach a lesson for the team. Some volunteer first to "get it out of the way" while others opt to teach last after getting more familiar with the process. In teams where there are more members than opportunities to teach, the team usually works out a solution that feels fair to them, such as drawing straws to see who'll teach.

THREE VARIATIONS TO THE LAUNCH AGENDA

Now that we've delved into the specifics of what we cover in the team launch agenda, I expect readers to ask, "Is it possible to do all this in one day?"

The answer is yes and no. It depends.

In most districts, I've launched the process in one day. With this tight, efficient agenda, we leave at the end of the day ready for lesson one. Efficiency allows us to focus more of our collaborative time on observing and debriefing student learning together. In comparison to lesson study, we spend less time up front designing our approach and more time in classrooms testing and refining it together.

That said, when additional time is possible, we take advantage of it to extend time teachers collaborate to design formative assessment tasks and/or plan instruction. Depending on the context, resources, and complexities of a team's goals, consider adjusting the launch agenda with one of the variations detailed in the next section. The first two are specific to increasing time, and the third introduces a shift in the workshop sequence.

Launch Variation 1: Extend the Planning Time

The collective lesson planning time for the first launch day is short. It works for many teams, and some teams prefer to have more time to plan together. There can be tremendous variations in how much time a team needs to plan based on the following factors:

- Complexity of the POP
- Range of perspectives on the team
- If they are refining a lesson in a curriculum, or starting from scratch
- Whether this is the first lesson they plan together, or a follow-up in the inquiry cycle

A 60-minute planning window for the first lesson is in many ways "planning in real time" because while it feels short for creating the first lesson, 60 minutes is longer than teachers typically have to plan every lesson in a school day. One minute planning for every minute of instruction translates to a 12-hour workday—a reality most teachers have experienced and try not to repeat.

That said, planning collectively takes more time than planning alone because it takes time to discuss options, listen to different perspectives, and come to agreements about the task and strategies to use. It takes time to benefit from the rich contributions of diverse perspectives and then channel the discussion of options into a planning of specific lesson steps. If you can afford to schedule more time to plan together, take advantage of the opportunity to do so.

One agenda variation is to plan a follow-up meeting for lesson planning that will be within a week of when the team will teach and observe the lesson. It is easiest and most relevant to plan the specifics of the lesson close to the teaching date both to maximize connections with current classroom and to build on where students are presently in relation to the end goal.

Launch Variation 2: Add a Meeting to Analyze Student Work as Formative Data

As described in Chapter 4, it is valuable to create a pre- or postassessment task. On the first launch day this is part of the agenda for all teams. If the task is a written task, schedule follow-up meeting in which the team can collaborate to analyze student work from that task. If the task is dynamic and part of a live lesson, skip the work analysis meeting as the formative data team needs lives in the context of classroom learning. Plan that task as part of the first lesson to teach and observe together.

Launch Variation 3: Start With the Problem of Practice

Writing a POP is the one activity in the workshop agenda that I sometimes lead in a different order. This activity works well as planned as a midworkshop activity that launches team-specific planning. It also is powerful as the very first activity we begin with teachers *before* even introducing the what and how of engaging in inquiry around live lessons.

Starting with a POP establishes the "why" for launching team inquiry in a way that is very specific for teachers. It frames the purpose for our collective work, and often a sense of urgency for action, a key step for leading change (Kotter, 2012; Sinek, 2009).

The very first activities of the launch agenda also connect to the "why" for teachers, but in a different way. Consider making the "why" a more prominent first step by having teachers writing the POP before we even introduce the what and how of OI.

The primary advantage for writing the POP first is buy-in. It also helps a facilitator understand front and center what matters most to teams. When I start first with the POP, as always is my choice when an entire site will engage in OI, I listen and learn teams' data-driven priorities. Later, when introducing OI, I directly reference those priorities in my examples and explanation. The POPs teams have identified establish a powerful purpose I can build from as I invite teams to take the risk of engaging in a new form of collaboration in classrooms together.

With so many benefits of writing a POP first, why do I often include it later in the agenda? One advantage of writing the POP after introducing the process is teams often find it easier to write a specific POP and inquiry questions when they have an idea of how they will engage in inquiry around live lessons together. Another advantage is it is a logical first step in planning and sets a frame for the other activities in that stage of the workshop agenda.

Consider the following questions as you determine the best approach for your context:

- What processes do educators in your context already engage in to identify data-driven priorities and goals? How will you connect to this work?
- How do teachers feel about opening doors to collaborative inquiry around live lessons? Is it their fear or resistance that makes creating teams a challenge?
- Who will participate in learning teams? Will it be voluntary or expected?
- Are participating teams existing teams that collaborate in other contexts, or will they meet together for the first time on the launch workshop day?

APPENDIX B

Easy Protocol Reference

DEBRIEF A LESSON

Describe

1. Reread your notes, and choose five details relevant to the high-leverage challenge area and/or teacher's observation priorities.

2. Write each detail on a self-stick note.

3. Share your details with the team without adding any interpretation or judgment.

Tips

- The details are "talking chips." After sharing yours, listen until all others have shared.
- Avoid using adjectives that reflect positive or negative interpretation.
- If you hear a general or evaluative statement, ask, "What's the evidence?" "What student action did you see that lead to you that interpretation?"

Organize

1. Silently reread the different details on self-stick notes, and think of how to group similar data.

2. Collaborate to cluster the notes into groups or categories that illuminate trends.

Tips

- Group evidence in ways that help you answer team inquiry questions.
- Not all data clusters in trends. A piece of evidence may stand alone.
- Be open to diverse perspectives in how to organize the data. This is an open-ended task, and the actual organization is less important than the insights we gain from the data. Begin the next step of writing generalizations to capture all ideas.

Generalize

1. Make generalizations from the data about student actions, understandings, and abilities demonstrated in the lesson.

2. Choose a team member to write generalization statement on the board or chart paper.

Few students . . . Some students . . . Most students . . . All students . . .

2/20 students . . . No girls . . . When asked to _____, most students . . .

Tips

- Use qualifiers like "few," "some," or "all" to align generalizations to how many students participate in the lesson tasks.

Link Cause and Effect

1. Have each team member star up to three generalizations that are their top priorities to discuss as a team. Begin with the items that have stars, and address the others only if there is time and team interest.

2. For each generalization the team wants to repeat (e.g., student success), collaborate to identify instructional actions that directly lead to this outcome. The purpose is to articulate together how to replicate the success in other contexts.

3. For each generalization that represents a student challenge, brainstorm instructional actions the team can take to address that challenge in any classroom. Use copies of Note-Taking Template: Brainstorming Solutions to take notes.

Fifth, plan the next lesson

Tips

- For Step 2, think about actions observed in this lesson, actions that preceded this lesson, and actions any team member has seen achieve the same result.
- When addressing challenges, don't give feedback to the teacher who taught the lesson. Instead, talk about how to address the challenge when it comes up in any classroom. Ask, "What can *we* do to ensure students succeed with that challenge?"

Finally, set individual and team goals.

References

Armstrong, A. (2014). Build a culture that nurtures productive conflict. *Tools for Learning Schools, 17*(2), 1–3. Retrieved from http://learningforward.org/pub lications/tools-for-learning-schools/tools-for-learning-schools/2013/12/19/ tools-for-learning-schools-winter-2014-vol.-17-no.-2#.U2xsV179RMg.

Aud, S., Wilkinson-Flicker, S., Kristapovich, P., Rathbun, A., Wang, X., & Zhang, J. (2013). *The condition of education 2013*. Washington, DC. Retrieved from U.S. Department of Education: http://nces.ed.gov/pubs2013/2013037.pdf.

Barth, R. S. (2006). Improving relationships within the schoolhouse. *Educational Leadership, 63*(6), 8. Retrieved from http://www.ascd.org/publications/edu cational-leadership.aspx.

Boudett, K. P., City, E. A., & Russell, M. K. (2010). *Key elements of observing practice: A data wise DVD and facilitator's guide.* Cambridge, MA: Harvard University Press.

Bronson, P., & Merryman, A. (2010). The creativity crisis. *Newsweek*. July 10, 2010.

Bryk, A., Sebring, P. B., Allensworth, E., Luppescu, S., & Easton, J. Q. (2010). *Organizing schools for improvement: lessons from Chicago.* Chicago, IL: University of Chicago Press.

Chenoweth, K. (2009). *How it's being done: Urgent lessons from unexpected schools.* Cambridge, MA: Harvard Education Press.

Chokshi, S., & Fernandez, C. (2004). Challenges to importing Japanese lesson study: Concerns, misconceptions, and nuances. *Phi Delta Kappan, 85*(7), 520–525. Retrieved from http://www.kappanmagazine.org.

City, E. A., Elmore, R. F., Fiarman, S. E., & Teitel, L. (2009). *Instructional rounds in education: A network approach to improving teaching and learning.* Cambridge, MA: Harvard Education Press.

Covey, S. R. (2013). *The 7 habits of highly effective people: Powerful lessons in personal change* (25th Anniversary Edition). New York, NY: Simon & Schuster.

Del Prete, T. (2013). *Teacher rounds: A guide to collaborative learning in and from practice.* Thousand Oaks, CA: Corwin.

Dufour, R. (2004). What is a professional learning community? *Educational Leadership, 61*(8), 6–11. Retrieved from http://www.ascd.org/publications/ educational-leadership.aspx.

DuFour, R., DuFour, R., & Eaker, R. (2008). *Revisiting professional learning communities at work: New insights for improving schools.* Bloomington, IN: Solution Tree Press.

Dweck, C. S. (2006). *Mindset: The new psychology of success.* New York: Random House.

Dweck, C. S. (2008). *Mindset: The new psychology of success.* New York, NY: Ballantine Books.

Ermeling, B., & Gallimore, R. (2013). Learning to be a community: Schools need adaptable models to create successful programs. *Journal of Staff Development, 34*(2), 42–45. Retrieved from http://learningforward.org/publications/jsd#.U2xtqF79RMg.

Ermeling, B., & Graff-Ermeling, G. (2014). Learning to learn from teaching: A first-hand account of lesson study in Japan. *International Journal for Lesson and Learning Studies, 3*(2), 170–192.

Fang, Z., Schleppegrell, M., & Cox, B. (2006). Understanding the language demands of schooling: Nouns in academic registers. *Journal of Literary Research, 38*(3), 247–273.

Fast Company Staff. (2006, March 20). Design thinking . . . what is that? *Fast Company.* Retrieved from http://www.fastcompany.com/919258/design-thinking-what.

Fillmore, L., & Snow, C. (2000). *What teachers need to know about language.* Washington, DC: U.S. Department of Education. Retrieved from http://files.eric.ed.gov/fulltext/ED444379.pdf.

Firestein, S. (2012). *Ignorance: How it drives science.* New York, NY: Oxford University Press.

Friedman, T. L. (2005). *The world is flat: A brief history of the twenty-first century.* New York, NY: Farrar, Straus and Giroux.

Fujii, T. (2013, July). *The critical role of task design in lesson study.* Plenary session presented at the International Commission on Mathematical Instruction Study 22 Conference, Oxford, United Kingdom. Retrieved from http://www.mathunion.org/fileadmin/ICMI/files/Digital_Library/Studies/Fujii_Japan_ICMI_Study_FINAL_200130822.pdf.

Gallimore, R., Ermeling, B. A., Saunders, W. M., & Goldenberg, C. (2009). Moving the learning of teaching closer to practice: Teacher education implications of inquiry teams. *The Elementary School Journal, 109*(5), 537–553. Retrieved from http://www.jstor.org/stable/10.1086/597001.

Genesee, F., Lindholm-Leary, K., Saunders, W. M., & Christian, D. (Eds.). (2006). *Educating English learners: A synthesis of research evidence.* Cambridge, England: Cambridge University Press.

Gibbons, P. (2009). *English learners, academic literacy, and thinking: Learning in the challenge zone.* Portsmouth, NH: Heinemann.

Gleason, S. C., & Gerzon, N. (2013). *Growing into equity.* Thousand Oaks, CA: Corwin.

Goldenberg, C., & Coleman, R. (2010). *Promoting academic achievement among English Learners: A guide to the research.* Thousand Oaks, CA: Corwin.

Goleman, D., Boyatzis, R. E., & McKee, A. (2002). *Primal leadership: Realizing the power of emotional intelligence.* Boston, MA: Harvard Business School Press.

Haidt, J. (2006). *The happiness hypothesis: Finding modern truth in ancient wisdom.* New York, NY: Basic Books.

Hattie, J. (2012). *Visible learning for teachers: Maximizing impact on learning.* New York, NY: Routledge.

Heath, C., & Heath, D. (2010). *Switch: How to change things when change is hard.* New York, NY: Crown Business.

Heifetz, R. A., & Linsky, M. (2002). *Leadership on the line.* Cambridge, MA: Harvard Business School Press.

Heritage, B. M. (2007). Formative assessment: What do teachers need to know and do? *Phi Delta Kappan, 89*(02), 140–145. Retrieved from http://www.kappan magazine.org.

Hollins, E. R., McIntyre, L. R., DeBose, C., Hollins, K. S., & Towner, A. (2004). Promoting a self-sustaining learning community: Investigating an internal model for teacher development. *International Journal of Qualitative Studies in Education, 17*(2), 247–264. doi: 10.1080/09518390310001653899.

Hord, S. M. (Ed.). (2004). *Learning together, leading together: Changing schools through professional learning communities.* New York, NY: Teachers College Press.

IDEO. (2013). *Design thinking for educators* (2nd ed.). Retrieved from http://www .designthinkingforeducators.com/toolkit/.

Joyce, B., & Showers, B. (1980). Improving inservice training: The messages of research. *Educational Leadership, 37*(5).

Joyce, B., & Showers, B. (1981). Transfer of training: The contribution of "coaching." *Journal of Education, 163*(2), 163–172.

Kelly, D., Xie, H., Nord, C. W., Jenkins, F., Chan, J. Y., & Kastberg, D. (2013). *Performance of U.S. 15-year-old students in mathematics, science, and reading literacy in an international context: First look at PISA 2012* (National Center for Education Statistics 2014–024). Retrieved from https://nces.ed.gov/pubs 2014/2014024rev.pdf.

Killion, J. (2008). *Assessing impact: Evaluating staff development* (2nd ed.). Thousand Oaks, CA: Corwin.

Killion, J. (2013). *Establishing time for professional learning.* Oxford, OH: Learning Forward.

Killion, J., Harrison, C., Bryan, C., & Clifton, H. (2012). *Coaching matters.* Oxford, OH: Learning Forward.

Knight, J. (2011). *Unmistakable impact: A partnership approach for dramatically improving instruction.* Thousand Oaks, CA: Corwin.

Kotter, J. P. (2012). *Leading change.* Boston, MA: Harvard Business Review Press.

Kotter, J. P., & Cohen, D. S. (2012). *The heart of change: Real-life stories of how people change their organizations.* Cambridge, MA: Harvard Business Review Press.

Kouzes, J. M., & Posner, B. Z. (2009, January). To lead, create a shared vision. *Harvard Business Review 87*(1), 20–21. Retrieved from, http://hbr.org.

Lean Impact. (2014). About lean impact [Web page]. Retrieved from http://www .leanimpact.org/about-lean-impact/.

Learning Forward. (2011). *Standards for professional learning.* Retrieved from http://learningforward.org/standards/outcomes. Oxford, OH: Author.

Learning Forward. (2011, October 6). *Outcomes standard* [Video file]. Retrieved from http://learningforward.org/standards/outcomes#.U3abYV79RMh.

Lewis, C. (2002). *Lesson study: A handbook of teacher-led instructional change.* Retrieved from http://www.rbs.org/catalog/pubs/pd55.php.

Lewis, C. C., Perry, R. R., Friedkin, S., & Roth, J. R. (2012). Improving teaching does improve teachers: Evidence from lesson study. *Journal of Teacher Education, 63*(5), 368–375. doi:10.1177/0022487112446633.

Lewis, C., Perry, R., Hurd, J., O'Connell, M. P. (2006). Lesson Study Comes of Age in North America. *Phi Delta Kappan, 88*, 273–282. Retrieved from http://www .kappanmagazine.org/.

Lewis, C., Perry, R., & Murata, A. (2006). How should research contribute to instructional improvement? The case of lesson study. *Educational Researcher, 35*(3), 3–14. doi:10.3102/0013189X035003003.

Lindsey, R. B., Robins, K. N., & Terrel, R. D. (2009). *Cultural proficiency: A manual for school leaders.* Thousand Oaks, CA: Corwin.

Little, J. W. (2006). *Learning-centered school professional community and learning-centered school.* Retrieved from National Education Association website: http://www.nea.org/assets/docs/HE/mf_pdreport.pdf.

MacDonald, E. B. (2013). *The skillful team leader: A resource for overcoming hurdles to professional learning for student achievement.* Thousand Oaks, CA: Corwin.

Mitchell, S. N., Reilly, R. C., & Logue, M. E. (2009). Benefits of collaborative action research for the beginning teacher. *Teaching and Teacher Education, 25*(2), 344–349. doi:10.1016/j.tate.2008.06.008.

Moran, M. C. (2007). *Differentiated literacy coaching: Scaffolding for student and teacher success.* Alexandria, VA: Association for Supervision and Curriculum Development.

Murata, A. (2010). Teacher learning with lesson study. In Peterson, P., Baker, E., & McGaw, B. (Third Edition), *International Encyclopedia of Education* (pp. 575–581). doi:10.1016/B978–0-08–044894–7.00659-X.

NGSS Lead States. (2013). *Next generation science standards: For states, by states. Achieve, Inc. on behalf of the twenty-six states and partners that collaborated on the NGSS.* Retrieved from http://www.nextgenscience.org/trademark-and-copyright-guidelines.

OECD. (2013). *PISA 2012 results: Excellence through equity: Giving every student the chance to succeed* (Volume II). Retrieved from http://dx.doi.org/10.1787/9789264201132-en.

Pink, D. H. (2009). *Drive: The surprising truth about what motivates us* [CD]. New York, NY: Penguin Audio.

Rebora, A. (2013a, March 13). Charlotte Danielson on teaching and the Common Core [Weblog post]. Retrieved from http://www.edweek.org/tm/articles/2013/03/13/ccio_danielson_teaching.html.

Rebora, A. (2013b, December 11). Noguera: Educators must be 'guardians of equity' [Weblog post]. Retrieved from http://blogs.edweek.org/teachers/teaching_now/2013/12/dallas_at_the_outset_of.html.

Reis, E. (2011). *The lean start up: How today's entrepreneurs use continuous innovation to create radically successful businesses.* New York, NY: Crown Business.

Richardson, J. (2000, February/March). Teacher research leads to learning, action. *Tools for Schools, 3*(4), 1–6. Retrieved from http://learningforward.org/publications/tools-for-learning-schools/page/4#.U2xu2179RMg.

Santos, M., Darling-Hammond, L., & Cheuk, T. (2012). *Teacher development to support English Language Learners in the context of the Common Core State Standards.* Retrieved from Stanford University School of Education website: http://ell.stanford.edu/sites/default/files/pdf/academic-papers/10-SantosLDHTeacherDevelopment FINAL.pdf.

Saunders, W. M., Goldenberg, C. N., & Gallimore, R. (2009). Increasing achievement by focusing grade-level teams on improving classroom learning: A prospective, quasi-experimental study of Title I schools. *American Educational Research Journal, 46*(4), 1006–1033. doi:10.3102/0002831209333185

Schleppegrell, M. (2004). *The language of schooling: A functional linguistics perspective.* Mahwah, NJ: Lawrence Erlbaum.

Seelig, T. (2012). *InGenius: A crash course on creativity.* New York, NY: HarperCollins.

Showers, B. (1987). Coaching teachers: A conversation with Bruce Joyce. *Educational Leadership, 44*(5), 12–17. Retrieved from http://www.ascd.org/publications/educational-leadership.aspx.

Sinek, S. (2009). *Start with why: How great leaders inspire everyone to take action.* New York, NY: Penguin.

Stepanek, J., Appel, G., Leong, M., Mangan, M. T., & Mitchel, M. (2007). *Leading lesson study: A practical guide for teachers and facilitators.* Thousand Oaks, CA: Corwin.

Thurlings, M., Vermeulen, M., Kreijns, K., Bastiaens, T., & Stijnen, S. (2012). Development of teacher feedback observation scheme: Evaluating the quality of feedback in peer groups. *Journal of Education for Teaching: International Research and Pedagogy, 38,* 193–208.

Valdés, G., Kibler, A., & Walqui, A. (2014, March). *Changes in the expertise of ESL professionals: Knowledge and action in an era of new standards.* Alexandria, VA: TESOL International Association.

Vescio, V., Ross, D., & Adams, A. (2006, January). *A review of research on professional learning communities: What do we know?* Paper presented at the NSRF Research Forum, Denver, Colorado. Retrieved from http://www.nsrfharmony.org/research.vescio_ross_adams.pdf.

Wagner, T., (2012). *Creating innovators: The making of young people who will change the world.* New York, NY: Scribner.

Washburn, K. D. (2010). *The architecture of learning: Designing instruction for the learning brain.* Pelham, AL: Clerestory Press.

Watanabe, T., Takahashi, A., & Yoshida M. (2008). Kyozaikenkyu: A critical step for conducting effective lesson study and beyond. In F. Arbaugh & P. M. Taylor (eds.), *Inquiry into Mathematics Teacher Education,* pp. 139–142. San Diego, CA: Assocation of Mathematics Teacher Educators.

Wei, R. C., Darling-Hammond, L., Andree, A., Richardson, N., & Orphanos, S. (2009). *Professional learning in the learning profession: A status report on teacher development in the United States and abroad.* Dallas, TX: National Staff Development Council.

Wiggins, G., & McTighe, J. (2005). *Understanding by design* (2nd ed). Alexandria, VA: Association for Supervision and Curriculum Development.

Wiseman, L., with McKewon, G. (2010). *Multipliers: How the best leaders make everyone smarter.* New York, NY: HarperCollins.

Wong Fillmore, L. (2004, April). The role of language in academic development. Keynote address given at Closing the Achievement Gap for EL Students conference. Sonoma, CA.

Zwiers, J. (2008). *Building academic language: essential practices for content classrooms.* San Francisco, CA: Jossey-Bass.

Zwiers, J., & Crawford, M. (2011). *Academic conversations: Classroom talk that fosters critical thinking and content understandings.* Portland, ME: Stenhouse Publishers.

Zwiers, J., O'Hara, S., & Pritchard, R. (2014). *Common core standards in diverse classrooms: Essential practices for developing academic language and disciplinary literacy.* Portland, ME: Stenhouse Publishers.

Index

Note: In page references, f indicates figures.

Notes

Notes

Notes

Notes

CORWIN
A SAGE Company

Corwin is committed to improving education for all learners by publishing books and other professional development resources for those serving the field of PreK–12 education. By providing practical, hands-on materials, Corwin continues to carry out the promise of its motto: **"Helping Educators Do Their Work Better."**